The Chester to Denbigh Railway

By
Roger Carvell

Irwell Press Ltd.

Acknowledgements

The writer would like to thank A.F.W. Astle, Assistant Regimental Secretary, Chester Castle, Chris Bushell, Brian Cowlishaw, Ray Davies, Stuart Eastwood, Curator of The Border Regiment Museum, Carlisle, Richard Foster of the Signalling Record Society, Norman Kneale, H. Higgins, Mark Higginson of The Silk Mill (Derby Industrial Museum), Ron Hill, signalman, the late Owen J. Hughes, driver at Mold Junction, C. Hopwood of Synthite Ltd, Charlie Hulme, who runs the excellent North Wales Coast Railway website at www.nwrail.org.uk, Harry Jack of the London & North Western Society, Bryn Jones, Cleve Jones, Mold Jct fireman, the late Norman Jones FSCA, Norman Lee, H. Loundes, signalman, Jim Lowe, Michael Mensing, M.J.P. Mitchell, Norman Parker, Mark Pardoe of the GNR Society, the late Peter Roberts, A.J. Robinson, Brian Rumary, Keith Smith, Bill Stubbs, A.G. Veysey, Clwyd County Archivist, Sidney Wainwright, J.E. White, the late Emrys Williams, driver, Geraint Williams, Ken Williams of BAE Systems, Broughton and T. Whitehead of Corus Steel for their generous and kind assistance in preparing this book.

Mention should also be made of the staff at *Railnews* who kindly included space in 'the railwaymen's newspaper' for an appeal to serving and former staff to step forward with their memories of the Chester to Denbigh line.

Sources:The British Library Newspaper Library Colindale, for back issues of The Chester Chronicle, Flintshire County Herald, Flintshire Leader, North Wales Weekly News, Liverpool Daily Post and Echo, The House of Lords Record Office Westminster for the original Parliamentary records and deposited plans, The National Archives, Kew. for all references to the Chester to Denbigh line under RAIL.

Bibliography: *The Chester & Holyhead Railway* by Peter E. Baughan (David & Charles, 1972), *A Regional History of the Railways of Great Britain*, Vol 11, *North & Mid Wales* by Peter E. Baughan (David & Charles, 1980), *The North Wales Coast Railway* by Peter E. Baughan (Martin Bairstow, 1988), *Rails to North Wales* by S.D. Wainwright (Ian Allan, 1978), *Forgotten Railways, North and Mid Wales* by Rex Christiansen (David & Charles, 1976, 1984), *The Chester & Holyhead Railway* by J.M. Dunn (Oakwood Press, 1948), *The Wrexham, Mold & Connah's Quay Railway* by J.M. Dunn (Oakwood Press), *The Mold Riots* (Clwyd Record Office,1991), *An Historical Survey of Chester to Holyhead Railway* by V.R. Anderson and G.K. Fox (Oxford Publishing Co, 1984), *The Building of the Mold and Denbigh Junction Railway* by R.G. Williams, *The Sowing & The Harvest* by W.J.Crosland-Taylor reprint (Transport Publishing Ltd, 1982), articles by J.M. Dunn in the *Railway Magazine* for June and July 1962 and *Railway Observer* notes 1942 to date (RCTS), *Industrial Locomotives of North Wales* (The Industrial Railway Society, 1992), British Railways (LMR Western Division) 1955 Working Time Tables for Passenger Trains, BR (LMR) Working Timetables for Freight Trains on Chester and Holyhead branches, 1964 and 1969, *Welsh Place Names* by John Jones (John Jones Publishing Ltd, 1983), *Railways of North Wales, the Modern Era* by Trefor Thompson (T&M Thompson, 1982), Bradshaw's July 1922 Railway Guide reprint (Guild Publishing, 1988), *Industry in Clwyd* by C.J. Williams (Clwyd Record Office, 1986), *The Vale of Clwyd Railway* by Stephen P. Goodall (Stephen P. Goodall,1992) *The Lead Mines Of The Alyn Valley* by C.J. Williams (Flintshire Historical Society, 1987), *The Crewe Type* by D.H. Stuart and Brian Reed (Profile Publications, 1971), *BR Steam Shed Allocations, Part 10*, by P.B. Hands, (Defiant Publications 1987).

First published in the
United Kingdom in 2009
by Irwell Press Ltd.,
59A, High Street, Clophill,
Bedfordshire MK45 4BE

Printed by Konway Print House

Contents

Introduction   Page   1

Chapter 1   Page   3

Chapter 2   Page   9

Chapter 3   Page   13

Chapter 4   Page   15

Chapter 5   Page   17

Chapter 6   Page   21

Chapter 7   Page   29

Chapter 8   Page   35

Chapter 9   Page   43

Chapter 10   Page   45

Chapter 11   Page   55

Chapter 12   Page   61

Chapter 13   Page   67

Chapter 14   Page   81

Chapter 15   Page   91

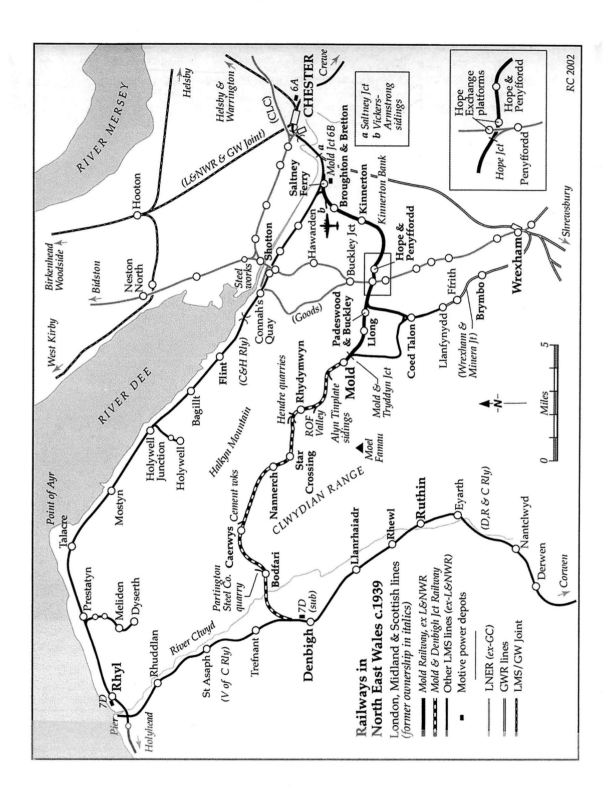

Railways in
North East Wales c.1939

London, Midland & Scottish lines
(former ownership in italics)

Mold Railway, ex L&NWR
Mold & Denbigh Jct Railway
Other LMS lines (ex-L&NWR)
Motive power depots

LNER (ex-GC)
GWR lines
LMS/GW Joint

Hope Exchange platforms
a Saltney Jct
b Vickers-Armstrong sidings

RC 2002

Introduction

While researching and writing this book about the Chester to Denbigh railway line I discovered that the process of acquiring historical information and then writing it up was rather like a train journey itself. Newly discovered information or photographs equalled the sense of excitement as the train pulled away from a station. Research took me through unfamiliar places. A friendly and helpful phone call from a former railwayman who knew the line in its heyday equated to the excitement of the train at speed. There were other times though, when the quest for completion seemed to grind to a halt as if the train had pulled up, unexpectedly, at a stop signal. Heads might appear at the window, wondering at the delay. Sometimes the reason was because material had to be acquired from a source which, perhaps, was not geared to devoting resources to events that occurred over 100 years ago.

Time, the great stealer, can encroach on an author's ambition, for middle aged writers have to make ends meet. But sooner or later the stop signal pulled off and the journey resumed its pace once more, as further nuggets of knowledge were discovered or a site visit undertaken. Then, as the last few paragraphs or captions are written, a distant signal is sighted at 'on' and the author knows it is time to zip up the travelling bag of railway history for now, and make ready to alight at the conclusion. In this railway history I have attempted to portray and bring to life once more, by study of the local press and official BR documents, the events that surrounded the Chester to Denbigh line through its 136 years of existence.

In truth, rural secondary lines like this one were overshadowed by the more glamorous – infamous, in its early years – Chester to Holyhead main line; contemporary railway authors and photographers found easier pickings among the expresses, seaside excursions and epic Victorian engineering that made up that strategic railway. Thus, little has appeared in print about another double-tracked railway, one that curved and twisted through the pleasant, rural, Alyn and Wheeler valleys and linked the Welsh county towns of Flintshire and Denbighshire with north-west England. However, as a North Wales railwayman once told me: 'the Denbigh line was very good, but too good to last.'

This is the story of that line.
Roger Carvell February 2009

Looking east towards Mold from the road overbridge at Rhyd-y-Goleu. The Synthite Works can be seen on the right with the Alyn Tinplate Works signal box in the middle distance. The River Alyn (responsible of breaching the line at this point in 1879) flows to the right of the telegraph pole in the foreground. Photograph Ray Davies.

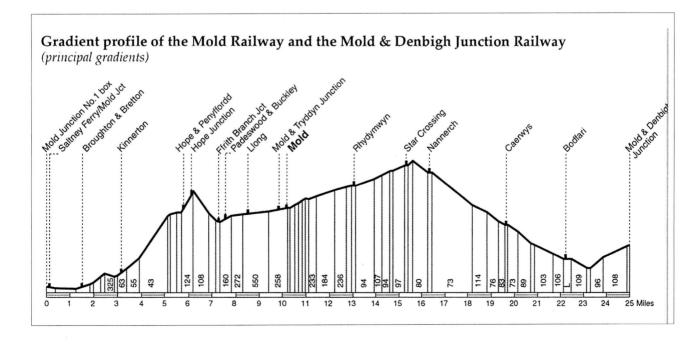

Gradient profile of the Mold Railway and the Mold & Denbigh Junction Railway
(principal gradients)

An **LNWR** Trevithick 2-4-0 tank No.284 in works grey paint. Engines such as these, in tender, and later tank engine form, formed the mainstay of the Mold branch services in the earliest years. One or two would have been stationed at Mold engine shed.

Chapter One
Coals to Industry: the Arrival of the Mold Railway

Late in 1985, demolition contractors completed lifting of the last remaining four and three quarter mile section of the former LNWR Chester to Denbigh branch line in North Wales. This, merely a truncated central portion of the original line, ran from Penyffordd, where a spur connected it with the ex-Great Central Wrexham-Bidston line, to the works of Synthite Ltd, a mile west of Mold. Since 15th March 1983, when the final working of chemical tank wagons made its way over the single track, freight only branch, the line had lain unused, and now its abandoned formation has been severed by the Mold eastern bypass. This final act of closure brought to an end the network of LNWR branch lines in the north-east corner of Wales, a system which extended from Chester (Saltney Ferry) to Mold and Denbigh and from Rhyl to Denbigh, Ruthin and Corwen. The area was rich in coal and other minerals at the eastern end, with the western portion devoted mainly to farming.

All these railways passed through pleasant, rolling countryside and a particularly delightful journey was from Chester to Mold, then onwards through the narrow, sylvan Alyn and Wheeler valleys to Denbigh, an original county town situated amid the flat lands of the Vale of Clwyd. The journey today is only possible by road but it is not difficult to trace on foot or recreate in the mind the double-tracked secondary line, which in part almost failed to get built at all but for the determination of the little-known Mold & Denbigh Junction Railway Company.

As early as 1825 a proposal had been made to build a railway linking the villages of Coed Talon and Treuddyn with the River Dee, culminating in a Mold Railway Bill, introduced into Parliament that year. However, opposition from the trustees of the turnpike road companies, who feared a loss of revenue, led to the Bill being dropped. But the demands of a growing industrial society, coupled with ever increasing volumes of trade, led to renewed pleas from colliery owners and townsfolk in the Mold district for a railway to link the town with the emerging national railway system. To give some idea of how slow communications were in the 1840s, gunpowder, brought by donkey from Stoke on Trent to the lead mines in the Mold district, involved the carrier in a round trip of six to seven days. At the same time, locally mined coal was laboriously transported away from collieries by horse and cart.

After some strong lobbying, there was disappointment in Mold when it was announced that the new railway from Chester to Holyhead was planned to follow the flat coastal strip of land bordering the River Dee, some six miles to the north of the town. In 1845, to counter the protests about being bypassed by the new main line, the Chester and Holyhead Railway Company proposed their own Mold branch. Diverging from the C&HR main line near Saltney, the line would have reached Mold via Broughton and Kinnerton but protestations from colliery owners forced the scheme's abandonment.

Despite this setback a new Mold Railway Bill, linking Mold with the Chester and Holyhead Railway near Chester, succeeded in Parliament on 9th July 1847. The newly formed Mold Railway Company was empowered to build a partially double-tracked branch line (with mineral branches) from a junction at Saltney Ferry on the newly-completed Chester to Bangor section of the C&HR. The authorised capital was £180,000 with the Mold company permitted to borrow on mortgage or bond any amount up to £60,000. Construction of the ten mile branch was undertaken by Edward Betts, whose tender of £146,130 had been accepted

Broughton and Bretton station in July 1953. The signalman, elbow on knee, can be discerned in the signalbox while he and the photographer await an up train.

The level crossing at Hope & Penyffordd looking south towards Hope and Wrexham, with the station on the left and the original Saxby & Farmer signal box on the right. The station footbridge was authorised in 1905 with an extension to the public right of way in 1910. Photograph Ray Davies Collection.

in February 1847. The contract stipulated that the line was to be finished by 31st December 1847. Betts had also been the contractor for two sections of the Chester & Holyhead, the latter company subscribing £30,000 to the completion of the Mold branch. Later Samuel Peto partnered Betts to complete the railway but in the meantime, lack of money threatened completion of the works. The Mold company found its finances ebbing away to the trustees of the local turnpike roads who demanded compensation. The Mold & Broughton and Kings Ferry Road Trusts were paid £1,000 and £500 respectively to compensate for loss of income when the railway opened.

Economies had to be made. A half mile mineral branch which would have crossed over the Chester & Holyhead line and terminated at a wharf on the River Dee was not built. The Chester & Holyhead, aware of the potential for coal traffic in the Mold district, became impatient at the slow rate of progress. In 1848 the line was still under construction and by agreement with the Mold board, the C&HR decided to purchase and complete the railway, together with the steeply-graded two and a quarter mile mineral branch from Ffrith Junction to Coed Talon. In order to save money, work on the section beyond Coed Talon to Ffrith was deferred, thus saving an estimated £5,000. This portion was eventually built 33 years later. The purpose of the branch to Coed Talon was to serve a number of collieries; connection with the

Nerquis Private Railway, also built to serve collieries in the country south of Mold, was made at Coed Talon.

The completed Mold branch was formally inspected on 19th July 1849 by Captain George Wynne R.E. for the Commissioner of Railways. In a report to the Commissioners dated 20th July 1849, Captain Wynne noted that the Mold Railway had a length of 10 miles, with 7 and a quarter miles as double line, the remaining distance into Mold being single. He found the line: '*In good order, the works well constructed and complete in every particular, with the exception of the signals, which were incomplete at the junction, at the stations, and at the terminus.*' He therefore refused permission for the line to open for public use until the signalling work was completed. A fortnight later, in a further report to Captain Harness R.E., Commissioner for Railways, Captain Wynne wrote:

'London, August 1st, 1849.

'Sir, I have the honour to report, for the information of the Commissioners, that yesterday I re-inspected the Mold Railway from its junction with the Chester and Holyhead Railway to the town of Mold, and I found that the signals which were not erected on my first inspection are now completed, and I am of opinion that the line may be opened with safety for the conveyance of passengers.

'I have &c.,

'GEORGE WYNNE,

'Capt. Royal Engineers.'

The Mold branch opened for traffic on 14th August and in a brief news item, the *Chester Chronicle* noted the advent 'of this important mineral tributary', and also mentioned the 'usual amount of dining and dancing' concurrent with the special trains that conveyed passengers along the line at reduced fares; at Mold the opening day was marked by a general holiday.

The inaugural timetable, published in the *Chester Chronicle*, listed two passenger trains a day each way between Mold and Chester throughout the week, including Sundays. The first, a 'Parliamentary train', arrived at Chester at 10.15 am, with the afternoon arrival (advertised as a third class train), arriving at 5 pm. Departures for Mold were at 10.45 am (Parliamentary) and at 6 pm (third class). A journey from Chester to Mold cost 2s 6d first class (no mention was made of any first class accommodation in the timetable) while the equivalent Parliamentary fare was 1s 1d. By October goods trains were advertised, such vehicles being attached to the timetabled passenger trains and an additional passenger train arrived at Chester from Mold at 1.10 pm with a return working at 3 pm.

The Chester & Holyhead Railway did not have any locomotives and coaching stock, the LNWR providing its own for all passenger and freight trains over the main line to Holyhead. By agreement the LNWR worked all traffic on the Mold branch from its opening. A single road locomotive shed was provided on the up side at Mold. Passenger trains from Chester to Mold served three intermediate stations, known originally as Broughton, Hope and Llong. These wayside stations, all equipped by 1872 with private sidings, were built to the design of Francis Thompson, architect to the Chester & Holyhead. Broughton was renamed Broughton Hall in April 1861. The station nameboards were changed again on 1st July 1908, losing 'Hall' and gaining '& Bretton'. Likewise, Hope added '& Penyffordd' with effect from 16th January 1912, avoiding any confusion with Hope in Derbyshire.

The Ffrith branch (with a maximum gradient of 1 in 33) opened for goods traffic in November 1849. Traffic in coal and oil (distilled from the locally mined cannel coal) grew quickly with heavier goods trains. 'Crewe Type' 2-4-0 locomotives were used initially but they could lose their grip on the 1 in 43 Kinnerton bank between Broughton and Hope. The introduction of new, and larger, more powerful Ramsbottom 'DX' 0 6 0s eased matters but throughout the history of the line, goods trains were banked when necessary up Kinnerton bank.

The steepness of the incline had not gone unnoticed on the Southern Division of the LNWR who saw it as an ideal testing ground for No.173, a Bury, Curtis & Kennedy 0-4-0 with 4ft driving wheels and 15in x 20in cylinders. In late 1849 No.173 was sent north from Wolverton Works in Buckinghamshire to the Mold branch but nothing is known of how it performed or to the exact date of the trials. No.173 is said to have been used at some stage on the

Leighton Buzzard to Dunstable branch which opened in 1848 and had a similar 1 in 40 incline.

Kinnerton bank was the scene of two known accidents in the 1850s. Both, reported by the Railway Inspectorate Department of the Board of Trade, involved trains running into each other, fortunately without loss of life. Indeed, compared with the parent Chester & Holyhead main line's accident record, the Mold branch appears to have escaped lightly with only the two BoT notified accidents prior to 1900.

The first accident occurred on 12th May 1856. A cattle train, comprising a tender locomotive, 36 cattle wagons, a second and a third class carriage, together with brake van left Mold at 2.30pm for Chester. Running half an hour late, the train passed Hope station at 2.53pm and then halted at the top of Kinnerton bank, in accordance with custom, to pin down sufficient wagon brakes to check the speed of the train on its descent of the 1 in 43 grade. Once restarted and half a mile below the summit, the brakesman noticed that the train had split in two with eighteen wagons, the carriages and brake van separated from the front portion.

Warned of the rearmost wagons breaking loose by some platelayers, the engine crew accelerated their part of the train away from the following wagons, now solely under the control of the hapless brakesman. However, finding the front portion of the train pulling away down the bank, the brakesman released his brake in the hope that the momentum gained downhill would give sufficient impetus to take his part of the

train over the short 1 in 300 rise at the foot of Kinnerton incline to the apparent safety of Broughton station.

Unfortunately the speed of the wagons was insufficient and after gaining some of the short ascent the wagons halted and then rolled back into the dip, unseen by a following train due to trees, several overbridges and the curvature of the track. Aware that a following train was due, the brakesman, accompanied by a police inspector of the Chester & Holyhead Railway, who had travelled with him from Mold, jumped from their brake van and, with a red flag, ran up the incline to the rear of the train to give further warning. The following train was made up of a locomotive, fifteen loaded coal wagons and brake van. It had left Padeswood at 2.45 pm (having waited for the cattle train to pass) and approached Hope station. Ahead, the cattle train could be seen passing through the station. Brought to a stand, the coal train then waited six minutes to give the preceding train time to 'get out of the way' as Captain Tyler's report to the Board of Trade put it. The driver was given due warning about the cattle train and allowed to restart. He then took his train to the top of the incline, there to stop for his brakesman to pin down the brakes of six of the rearmost wagons. Once in motion again, the coal train began to descend Kinnerton bank at a speed of three to four miles per hour, the driver prudent enough to apply his tender brake and to shut off steam to check the descent.

By the time the engine crew saw the platelayers' frantic warning signals the

Padeswood and Buckley station from an up Chester train. It was the only station on the line to have a booking office located on an overbridge. Photograph R.M. Casserley.

coal train's speed had risen to 15 mph. The fireman then crept along the engine's running plate (the locomotive was running tender first) to climb aboard the first wagon and pin down the brake. However the wooden brake blocks were badly worn and as the lever dropped to the bottom of its guard the fireman almost lost his footing and narrowly escaped being thrown off. Once he had safely returned to the footplate, the driver, having put the locomotive into reverse, made his way along the running plate and over the first wagon to pin down the brakes of the second and third wagons. After all these Wild West goings-on, at a point a mile and 1,320 yards from the summit and one and a half miles from the foot of Kinnerton bank, the driver then saw the cattle train (front portion) proceeding to Broughton. Unaware of the stationary wagons hidden from view in the dip and assuming that all was well with the cattle train, he put the locomotive in back gear once more but did not release the tender brake. Rounding the curve, he then saw the stranded wagons and carriages 1,000 yards ahead. He immediately put the engine in reverse once more, but despite the combined brake force of ten wagons (the brakesman had succeeded in putting on a further wagon brake) and the retarding effect of the steam acting on the locomotive's coupled wheels, it was impossible to stop. Both driver and fireman leapt to safety as the coal train travelling at about 8-10 mph crashed into the stationary vehicles. Six or seven cattle dealers, travelling in the two carriages, were hurt by the impact and to quote Captain Tyler, 'the cattle suffered considerably'.

In his report to the Railway Inspectorate Department of the Board of Trade, Captain Tyler observed that no blame could be attached to any of the parties concerned in the collision, for none of the regulations regarding the time interval between the two trains had been breached. However, he criticised the running of such heavy trains, following each other at an interval of only a few minutes over the sort of gradients found between Hope and Broughton. He suggested the introduction of the telegraph between the stations concerned: 'Not allowing any train to leave the former until the line has been reported from the latter to be clear after the passage of a preceding train.'

The coal train was described in the C&H working timetable as a special train and was subject to the following company notice: 'As there is no exact time fixed for the running of coal trains on the Mold branch, it will be needful for every one concerned to keep a good look out, and be prepared for their arrival at any time.' Captain Tyler was also concerned about precautions regarding the adequacy (or lack of) braking power in proportion to the loads worked over 'this dangerous part of the line'. The driver of the coal train stated that: 'I never can stop that train when half way down the bank; sometimes it pushes us to the Mold Junction (nearly two and three quarters of a mile beyond the bottom of the incline) before we can pull up. We went down there on Friday night last. We then passed Broughton station at twenty miles an hour, although we had the brakes pinned down so that we could not start from the top. The same thing happened scores of times, when the rails are wet.'

Captain Tyler found that in addition to a requirement for a greater increase in braking power when descending Kinnerton bank he also found it desirable that in future all trains should be directed to stop at Broughton station. His final observation was that the coal train locomotive was travelling tender first and commented that this mode of working engines increased the liability to accidents 'of another nature', particularly on gradients such as those described above.

Wet rails were to be a contributory factor in the second collision to occur on Kinnerton bank just over eighteen months later. On 11th December 1857 a train of 14 empty wagons and brake van left Mold Junction at 9.10am for Padeswood station, headed by the regular engine that worked mineral traffic over the branch. The train proceeded satisfactorily until it reached a point a mile short of the summit of Kinnerton bank. A recent rain shower caused the locomotive to slip and while the fireman was engaged in sanding the rails, the empty wagon train was run into by the following 9.15 am Chester to Mold passenger train. This was headed by a tank locomotive which climbed Kinnerton bank at some 20-25 mph. Once again the curvature of the track prevented the driver from having a clear view of the obstruction ahead. Despite whistling for the guard's brake, putting the locomotive into reverse and applying the 'tender brake' the locomotive ploughed into the rear of the empty wagon train, derailing two wagons and slightly injuring two passengers. Little damage was caused to the passenger train.

Lt Col Yolland, in his report to the Railway Department of the Board of Trade on 2nd January 1858, noted that the driver of the empty wagon train asserted that, despite the wet rails and the consequent slipping of his locomotive, his train, at the time of the collision, was still moving at a rate of between four to six miles an hour. He also stated that the locomotive had sufficient steam and that it had been blowing off steam as they ascended Kinnerton bank. In contrast, the passenger train driver claimed that he thought the train of empty wagons was standing still at the time of impact. Lt Col Yolland duly wrote: 'The driver of the passenger train estimated his speed at the moment of collision at two miles an hour, and thus, according to the evidence, we are presented with the anomaly of a train travelling at two miles an hour, overtaking and running into another travelling at double that rate.' Yolland also remarked that 'the engine of the passenger train was a tank engine, with the water over the whole length of the boiler, and in consequence not favourable for the driver seeing what is on the line before him.'

This implied a saddle tank but Yolland does not record the identity of the engine concerned. The Chester and Holyhead Railway's regulations stated that the load to be taken up Kinnerton bank was left to the judgement of the brakesman who also decided whether the train should precede or follow a passenger train. Lt Col Yolland was critical of the practice of sending a preceding goods train, at the full weight which the locomotive could draw, up a five mile incline on a wet day. He recommended that the train of empty wagons should not be permitted to precede the passenger train, unless started fifteen minutes in advance. He further recommended that in all such cases the Station Master at Broughton should inform the passenger train driver that a train of empty wagons was ahead of him. It was further urged that a greater margin should be left between the absolute power of the engine and the load sent up the incline.

These early Board of Trade accident reports give a valuable insight into how Britain's earliest standard gauge railways were worked. With no intermediate signalling between stations and junctions, trains were expected to make their own way as best they could, in all weathers, protected only by an interval of time from other trains. Semaphore signals that did exist were often poorly sited and confined to stations and junctions. Railway employees were often lax in maintaining strict operating practices and confusion often arose over who was responsible for what in the safe conduct of rail traffic.

In the 1850s the Chester and Holyhead section of the LNWR had gained a certain notoriety. The frequent accidents, often in the sort of circumstances outlined above, did little to raise the confidence of the travelling public. Board of Trade inspecting officers continually urged the installation of the train telegraph between stations. They also pressed for the introduction of the absolute block signalling system in place of the increasingly dangerous time interval practice. It took the Abergele disaster of 1868, in which 33 passengers and the fireman of the down Irish Mail were burned to death in a head-on crash with runaway paraffin wagons, to bring public pressure to bear on the LNWR to improve safety. Improvements began in 1869. In February the train telegraph was ordered to be installed throughout the C&H and it was in place at Mold in June that year. The absolute block system of signalling was adopted in October 1870 and introductory work proceeded rapidly, at least on the C&H main line. The Annual Returns to the Board of Trade for 1873 (as required under the Regulation of Railways Act of 1873) showed that trains over the Mold branch and beyond were still being signalled by telegraph with the notable exception of the Broughton Hall to Hope section which was now signalled under absolute block regulations, no doubt because of the incline.

Even after the abolition of time interval working, semaphore signals interlocked with points could not offer complete safety. In 1872 advances in signalling work had led to the Mold Junction to Saltney Junction section of the C&H being worked under permissive block rules. On 11th April that year the 7.25 am Chester to Mold passenger train crashed into a goods train being shunted at Proctor and Rylands siding, east of Mold Junction. The passenger train driver had observed a caution signal at Saltney Junction indicating that the line ahead was blocked by a preceding train but had neglected to do anything about it. He then failed to notice or acknowledge the next signal, set at danger. In clear weather and at a speed of 20-25 mph, the locomotive ploughed into the rearmost wagons of the goods train, left standing on the down line while shunting was in progress. Three wagons were derailed and severely damaged while the brake van and one other wagon sustained some damage. None of the six passenger vehicles of the Mold train was derailed although the locomotive was damaged. One passenger was hurt in the leg while the guard was knocked over in his van, receiving cuts to the head and nose.

In his report for the Board of Trade, written at Chester on 23rd April, Lt Col Rich could give no account as to why the driver, of good character and in the LNWR's employ as a fireman and relief driver for six to seven years, had run into the goods train. Despite both signals, within a mile of each other, warning him of a preceding train, the driver had neglected to acknowledge their meaning and had run into the goods train at almost full speed. Lt Col Rich could only ascribe to the driver (who had subsequently been dismissed) 'a total absence of mind'.

The first signal boxes, erected by the signalling contractors Saxby and Farmer, did not appear on the Mold branch until 1875. Brick-built signal boxes opened that year at Hope, Mold & Tryddyn Junction and Mold. However, at least two more years were to pass before the entire line from Saltney Ferry to Denbigh was converted to absolute block working, in 1877-1878. The Mold Junction to Tryddyn Junction section was so dealt with by 31st December 1877. On the Coed Talon branch, time interval working continued in use over the double line section between Padeswood Junction and Coppa and indeed remained so until closure in the 1930s.

Despite the rapid growth of traffic over the Chester & Holyhead main line and its branches, the C&H's finances were still rocky; fearing a possible GWR take-over, the LNWR purchased the Chester & Holyhead Railway with effect from 1st January 1859, thus bringing the main line and the Mold branch wholly into the LNWR network.

The Mold branch was to enjoy a boom period in coal and oil traffic which lasted for over twenty years until

cheaper American oil imports in the 1870s caused a rapid decline in oil production. There were numerous colliery branches and sidings off the Mold branch. At Padeswood, a spur curved northwards to serve Nant Branch Colliery Co. Another colliery branch, again reaching out to the north, was recorded in a 1876 LNWR survey as the Twyddyn Branch. It opened in 1866 to serve the Bronwylfa Colliery as well as a brick and tile works. This outlet was located a quarter of a mile south of Mold & Tryddydn Junction. Records show that the colliery closed in October 1877. The Bromfield Colliery, with three shafts, on the southern outskirts of Mold, grew to be the largest colliery in the Mold district, employing over 400 miners at the time of its closure in June 1916. Coal had been mined at the Bromfield site since the 1830s and though flooding closed the pit in the 1850s it was revived and modernised between 1904 to 1905 by the Pontybodkin Colliery Co Ltd. The re-opened colliery's new 'merry-go-round' network of loading sidings was located adjacent to Mold and Tryddyn Junction; connection to LNWR metals was made via a trailing connection (crossing Gas Lane) to Mold's goods yard on the down side of the Mold branch. Prior to the laying of new sidings to the colliery, it had been served by a tramway. An 0-4-0 saddle tank, built by Hawthorn Leslie (works No.2646) in 1906 was supplied new to the colliery, now owned by Mold Collieries Ltd. Named 'Bromfield', it shunted wagons within the colliery and after closure languished at Mold until November 1918 when it passed to the Teeside Bridge Engineering Company of Middlesbrough.

Next door to the Bromfield Colliery were sidings (in existence by 1882) belonging to the Mold Gas & Water Company who possessed 'Dee', an Andrew Barclay 0-4-0 saddle tank (works No.1179 of 1910). Rebuilt in 1924 by Kerr Stuart, 'Dee' originated from ICI at Billingham and was used until 1948 when the owners (now the Wales Gas Board) purchased a replacement road tractor; 'Dee' was scrapped on site in May 1950. As well as coal and oil, sand traffic was dealt with at Dodd's Sand siding, located on Kinnerton bank. The sand, to be used for casting, was extracted from two quarries near Kinnerton Mill; a horse tramway made connection with a LNWR siding on the down side of the Mold branch.

Padeswood station, with its booking office on a road overbridge, opened for business in 1851. To reflect the growing importance of nearby Buckley as a brick and tile manufacturing centre, the station was renamed Padeswood & Buckley as from 1st February 1894. In 1891 further stations opened at Saltney Ferry (adjacent to the newly constructed Mold Junction engine shed) and at Kinnerton, where land owned by the Duke of Westminster was given to permit the building of the new station.

Llong station, between Padeswood and Mold, apparently deserted on a June 1959 day. This station closed twice: once during the First World War and permanently from 28 April 1962. Close to the River Alyn, it served little more than a few cottages. Signals and road crossing gates were controlled from a ground frame, manned by a porter/signalman. A pair of LNWR station huts provide the waiting accommodation on the up platform. Photograph Mowat Collection.

A Webb 2-4-2T approaches the Blue Hand Bridge, between Bodfari and Mold & Denbigh Junction with a Denbigh train on 12 September 1921. The change from a falling grade of 1 in 108 to a climb of 1 in 96 is apparent but the engine has steam to spare. The train is composed of six-wheel coaches. Photograph D.S. Foulkes Roberts.

An early, undated view of Nannerch station looking towards Bodfari. Beyond the road bridge a signal post signalling trains in both directions can just be made out. The uppermost arm is cleared for a train approaching from the Denbigh direction. The pointwork at the end of the platform leads to the cattle dock siding. No signal box was provided at Nannerch; the station lever frame can be seen to the right of the brick built outhouse on the right.

Chapter Two
Protracted Delay: The Mold and Denbigh Junction Railway

For twenty years passenger trains terminated at Mold but as far back as 1845 sections and plans had been prepared for a continuation of the Trent Valley line from Stafford through Whitchurch, Wrexham and Mold, to the small village of Bodfari. Here the line would have swung coastwards to form a junction with the Chester & Holyhead at a point between Rhyl and Abergele. Nothing came of this proposal, but in 1852 fresh initiative was given to a projected railway from Mold to Denbigh and Ruthin, the promoters hoping for the backing of the Chester & Holyhead. However the latter company, financially exhausted after the bridging of the River Conway and the Menai Straits, felt unable to assist a lesser cause and plans to reach Denbigh from Mold were therefore shelved.

In 1856 the Vale of Clwyd Railway was incorporated to build a ten mile single track branch from Rhyl (Foryd) southwards to Denbigh. The flat countryside surrounding the River Clwyd presented few problems for the builders and trains commenced running in October 1858. With Denbigh now on the railway map, extension of the line further inland came in 1864 with the opening of the Denbigh, Ruthin and Corwen Railway; again single track and connecting with the GWR at Corwen.

In 1861 the Mold & Denbigh Junction Railway, supported by the LNWR, was incorporated to build a railway between the two towns. There were five directors of the M&DJR – Richard Thomas Rowley, Llewelyn Falkner Lloyd, William Reynolds, Charles Butler Clough and George Moore Dixon. The address of the Company was 134 Palmerston Buildings, Bishopsgate Street, London and the first Board meeting took place on 24th August 1861.

The prospect of travelling through the beautiful Wheeler valley now looked more promising. However, at the 1861 Parliamentary hearing into the M&DJ Bill, opposition from influential landowners and both the Vale of Clwyd and Denbigh, Ruthin & Corwen railways, who feared a drain of traffic to the new line, led to the Bill being thrown out. Interestingly, the most notable initial objector was William Barber Buddicom, formerly Locomotive Superintendent of the Grand Junction Railway and latterly of the Paris-Rouen Railway. Buddicom, of Penbedw Hall, Nannerch, claimed that the proposed railway would 'damage his estates unnecessarily'. It is ironic that Buddicom, having made a fortune building locomotives in France, should object to the view from Penbedw Hall being spoilt by a railway!

The jubilant Vale of Clwyd Railway, when asked the reason for the rejection of the M&DJ Bill by Parliament, claimed that it was a case of a large company (the LNWR) oppressing a smaller one – the LNWR had paid the M&DJ's Parliamentary deposit of £10,000. Strange then that at the same time as the M&DJ Bill was before Parliament, the Vale of Clwyd Railway should be in the lobby, negotiating with the LNWR for the transfer of their line to Euston! Learning that this transfer had been confirmed, the Chairman of the House of Lords Committee urged the defeated M&DJ to re-commit their Bill, providing the objections of the landowners could be met. At great effort and expense the M&DJ overcame the objectors (a raised bank, planted with trees hid the permanent way from Buddicom's view together with a re-aligned carriage drive and new lodge for Penbedw Hall). In the same Parliamentary session the M&DJ Bill was passed, only the second railway Bill to have gone through this sequence of events up to that time.

Thus the M&DJ was empowered to build a 14¾ mile double track line from an end-on connection with the Mold branch to Denbigh on the now LNWR-controlled Vale of Clwyd branch. The Bill also included a three mile cut-off line that would have bypassed Denbigh to the east, diverging at Bodfari and forming a junction with the Denbigh, Ruthin & Corwen Railway at a point south of Denbigh though this line, at Euston's insistence, was never built. Elation was short-lived, for the LNWR, despite having originally backed the M&DJ, refused to undertake construction. Having gained one route

Caerwys station in its earliest years. The staff appear to have been carefully posed by the photographer, the porter/signalman (left) leaning against the hand operated lattice-post signal. This signal, like others initially supplied to the Mold & Denbigh Junction Railway, were manufactured by Stevens & Son of London. The low platform height and the ballast covering the sleepers are noteworthy. Photograph Ray Davies Collection.

Nannerch station after renewal and raising of the platforms, about 1900. The siding on the left led to a landing and the new down starter signal (centre) replaced an earlier one situated beyond the road bridge, from where the photograph was taken. Nannerch's signals were operated from a platform ground frame containing eight levers. A two lever frame gave access to the goods yard (behind the station building) and a third containing three levers operated the station crossover. All three frames were released by Annetts key. Photograph Ray Davies Collection.

to Denbigh (incidentally pre-empting any GWR desires to reach Rhyl from Corwen) Euston saw little point building a second line, passing through a thinly populated valley of pasture and woodland. So, for the next three years the M&DJ remained a 'paper' railway.

In 1864, with the prospect of their Parliamentary powers lapsing, the Mold company 'in a state of absolute alarm' approached Samuel France, a wealthy Shrewsbury contractor, with an offer to him to construct the line. Starting with a capital of £160,000 and backed by the Warrant Finance Company, France with George Bellis of Mold as engineer, quickly obtained the necessary land before the powers expired. France accepted preference shares in lieu of payment. Land was required a mile north of Denbigh for a triangular junction with the Vale of Clwyd line, but France found that the M&DJ Act made no mention of running powers over the final mile into Denbigh itself. There then came a period of quarrelling with the LNWR over access to Denbigh, which led to the by now exasperated Mold company building its own embankment into Denbigh from the authorised south junction.

Undaunted by the initial three year difficulty in getting the M&DJ built (the general public had taken up few shares) between 1864 and 1866 the company proposed several Bills for branch lines in the Mold area, none of which came to fruition. For the 1866 Parliamentary session, John Ashdown, acting jointly with George Bellis as engineers, planned no fewer than nine new branch lines radiating from Mold and Denbigh.

Noteworthy was a proposal for a three and a half mile line from Rhydymwyn which would curve south-eastwards to Loggerheads, a popular beauty spot set among limestone cliffs. Other schemes would serve Ewloe and collieries at Soughton and Argoed to the north-west of Mold. The most significant proposal (one that showed how strained relations were with Euston) was a new railway parallel with the Mold branch. This would then curve north-east to form a junction with the Wrexham, Mold and Connah's Quay railway at Spon Green near Buckley. This plan (which was passed by Parliament) would have given the M&DJ a link towards England without having to use the LNWR. From this line a two mile branch would diverge south-eastwards, crossing over the Mold branch to serve Nerquis Colliery. At Denbigh a new line would avoid Denbigh station and connect with the Denbigh, Ruthin and Corwen Railway. From the town a five mile branch would wend south-westwards to the village of Nant Glyn.

The most ambitious project was an 1866 plan for a 22 mile line diverging westwards from the Vale of Clwyd branch at Trefnant, curving through sparsely populated hills south of Abergele, bridging the Chester and Holyhead main line west of Colwyn Bay and terminating at Vaughan Street, Llandudno. However, caution prevailed over ambition amongst the company directors and the Llandudno Bill was withdrawn. On 4th August 1865, Bellis, in an engineer's report to the directors, stated that a single line of nine miles had been laid from Mold, with five and a half miles completed as double track and four and a half miles ballasted and ready for traffic. Despite this promising progress, 1866 brought another blow, for France's money dried up in the financial crash of that year and, with the line almost complete, work ceased.

While the M&DJ remained in limbo, 1866 also saw the opening of the Wrexham, Mold & Connahs Quay Railway which bridged the Mold branch near Penyffordd. To facilitate interchange, the LNWR opened a new station called Hope Junction with two platforms linked by a footpath to the then single platform of the WM&CQR. The WM&CQ Act made provision for north and south connecting spurs with the Mold line here but only the south facing one was completed, thus enabling through running from Wrexham to Mold, although in practice no timetabled passenger trains ever used it. Hope Junction station was renamed Hope Exchange in 1877. Relations between the LNWR and the WM&CQR were cordial and in 1886, construction of a south to east curve began at Penyffordd to enable through running from Chester via Hope to Wrexham. However, the WM&CQ then fell into the orbit of Sir Edward Watkin and the Manchester, Sheffield & Lincolnshire Railway. As there was little love lost between the M&SL and the LNWR, the earthworks were promptly abandoned.

Meanwhile the inert M&DJ lay unfinished for two years until late 1868 when a scheme was obtained in Chancery to raise capital to complete the railway. Samuel France parted company with the M&DJ, having a reached an amicable agreement with the Board on 5th November 1868. Work resumed on 7th December 1868, the new contractors being Messrs Scott & Edwards of Wigan, with George Bellis once again engineer. The lengthy period of inactivity had led to a deterioration in the state of works already completed. Of particular concern was Blue Hand Bridge, a road overbridge west of Bodfari. Mr France had attended a board meeting on 30th April 1868 and explained that 'the bridge had been put in a safe condition as far as the public going over the same were concerned but that it would have to be partly taken down and rebuilt'. At the end of the year nothing appeared to have been done about the bridge and it was resolved at a board meeting held on 5th November 1868 'to construct a temporary bridge at the Blue Hand, the existing bridge on the line at that point being in a dangerous state'.

The contract for building the wayside stations at Rhydymwyn, Nannerch, Caerwys and Bodfari was given to Messrs Hughes & Son of Rhyl. All were of substantial construction and quite different in style from Francis Thompson's stations on the Mold branch. The heaviest earthworks were west of Bodfari where a half mile cutting led onto an embankment of similar length. Road and rail bridges were built from limestone. Bellis informed the directors that given fair weather the line would be ready for traffic by May 1869. Late 1868 also saw the LNWR agreeing to work the M&DJ as if it were part of its own system, taking 50 per cent of the traffic receipts between Mold and Denbigh and 75 per cent from traffic originating elsewhere. After much legal argument this was later reduced to 50 per cent. The agreement also led to the M&DJ selling their embankment at Denbigh to the LNWR for £700 who then abandoned it, obliging the Mold company to double, at its own expense, the Vale of Clwyd branch into Denbigh, a distance of one mile. This in turn led to a delay in opening the line completely between Mold and Denbigh and it was not until 14th August 1869 that Bellis reported by letter to the directors that the line was ready for inspection by the Board of Trade.

Letter to: P.P. Pennant, Brynbella, Bodfari, G.M. Dixon, Bucknowle House, Wareham, Dorset; A.J. Roberts, Coed du, Mold; F.A. Hamilton, Founders' Court, Lothbury, London:

'Mold & Denbigh Junction Rly Co.,
Engineer's Office
Mold
14th August 1869
'Gentlemen, I have the satisfaction of reporting that your Railway is now so far completed that it will be ready for the inspection of the Government Inspector on Monday the 23rd instant.
'I am happy to say that the works on the line, including the stations have been executed in a substantial manner.

'It has taken more time to complete the line than was expected but a considerable portion of the delay has been caused at the Denbigh end in the doubling of the Vale of Clwyd Railway. This work was to have been done by the LNWR Co. but by a recent arrangement with that company it was undertaken by yourselves.
'I have the honour to be, Gentlemen, Your obedient servant,
George Bellis, Engineer.'

Bellis had earlier reported that he had obtained a turntable for £150 which the LNWR, at their own expense, would install at Denbigh. Upon formal inspection, Lt Col Hutchinson for the Board of Trade found work incomplete on deviated roads and refused permission to open the line. He also expressed dissatisfaction with Mold station, finding the station clock and nameboard missing. After his second inspection on 4th September 1869 Hutchinson gave his sanction for opening as from Monday, 6th September. In his initial report, compiled at Ripon in Yorkshire, he remarked that there were twenty bridges under the line and fourteen over. As the route closely followed much of the old Denbigh coach road, he recommended the erection of wooden screens on the underbridges near Rhydymwyn to prevent horses taking sudden fright when trains passed above the road.

A few weeks prior to the opening of the Mold and Denbigh Junction Railway, a violent event took place at Mold station that shook North Wales and made national news. In the late 1860s industrial unrest in the collieries had begun to grow. Colliers protested at poor working conditions while colliery owners, to stimulate demand, cut coal prices and consequently lowered miners' wages. Colliers, in turn, had much resentment towards outsiders taking their work. Trouble was particularly bad at Leeswood Green colliery where it was announced that coal prices would be cut as from 17th May 1869. This incensed the colliers and violence erupted on the 19th May. The colliery manager – a Durham man – was confronted by about fifty men as he took refuge in the engine house. Unable to reason with the crowd which had swelled to five or six hundred, he was dragged out, kicked and then frog-marched to Hope Junction station, there to be put on a train with a one-way ticket. This was the practice of 'sending a man packing', a tradition in the coalfields. At Hope Junction the unfortunate manager was met by two police constables who gave him safe passage to Mold. But the trouble continued, summonses for assault being issued for the alleged ringleaders while at Leeswood colliery a further riot took place on 24th May. Eventually eight colliers surrendered to the police and duly appeared at the Court House in Mold on 2nd June. A crowd of men, women and children, estimated at between 500 to 1,500, assembled outside the Court to await news of the sentences passed.

The authorities were prepared for trouble. A detachment of fifty soldiers arrived by train from Chester Barracks to reinforce the Flintshire Constabulary. When sentencing was complete there was uproar at the severity of the punishment. Some colliers were fined but two were each sentenced to one month's hard labour at Flint Gaol. As the two prisoners were marched under both military and police escort to the awaiting train, the protesters started jeering and began throwing stones. Confusion and fright swept through the English soldiers as the rioters shouted and booed in both English and Welsh. Women gathered stones in their aprons from the newly completed Tyddyn Street which overlooked Mold station. The station itself had been sealed off except for a narrow gate leading on to the platform. The Chester Street road overbridge also gave the stonethrowers the advantage of height and the air became black with stones, some weighing between 4 and 5lb, raining down on the station where carriage windows of the prisoners' train were shattered. The station buildings also suffered damage with many windows smashed; a wheelbarrow load of stones was later recovered from the vicinity of the station telegraph office.

Soldiers and constables stumbled and fell, badly injured and bleeding from the barrage of missiles. As they struggled through the entrance, only one police constable turned to face the crowd and throw back the stones. The commanding officer did not have the necessary magistrate's permission so was reluctant to give the order to fire at the rioters. But as the stonethrowers advanced upon the station platform, a magistrate from Chester, taking refuge in the front part of the train, gave the order to fire. An estimated fifteen shots were fired from the station precincts, killing one rioter instantly and fatally injuring three others – two of them women. As the shots rang out the angry crowd dispersed, leaving a carpet of stones and pools of blood on the station forecourt. As doctors treated the badly injured and dying, a further detachment of 100 soldiers were quickly despatched from Chester to restore and maintain order at Mold.

Thus ended what became known as the Mold Riots, an isolated and bloody event whose consequences are outside the scope of this book. Of significance to the military was the tactical advantage of rapidly moving soldiers and their equipment by rail, a tactic in which the Mold branch had played its part.

An old postcard view of Mold station. On the right an open top Milnes-Daimler omnibus awaits passengers. These vehicles pioneered early railway-operated motor services. The goods yard crane appears to be busy handling large consignments of raw timber. Visible beyond the crane is the upper portion of the original Saxby & Farmer signal box which stood on the up side of the line.

Sarn Mill, Ysceifiog, about 1912 looking north. The rails of the Mold & Denbigh line can be seen in the foreground. The village of Ysceifiog, with its fish hatcheries, was a popular destination for ramblers and day excursionists. The village itself was some way from the railway (and uphill) as visitors found after alighting at Caerwys station but the narrow, hedged roads offered pleasant views of rural pasture and moorland.

Chapter Three
The M&DJ Opens for Business - At Last

The 'Chester Chronicle', in a report on the line's opening, gave details of an excursion from Denbigh to Mold that ran as early as 1st September, three days before Lt Col Hutchinson's second inspection! Services were due to start on the 6th. The excursion was regarded as the inaugural train, run in connection with Mold's annual sports day, arriving at 11am. Mold was in festive mood, shops closing early and flags flying above the streets. A lunch was held in the Market Hall for the line's workmen. In the evening, the Black Lion Hotel hosted a public dinner at which Mr J. Scott Banks, High Sherriff, proposed a toast to the prosperity of the Mold & Denbigh Junction Railway and hoped that:

'In future the church clock and the railway clock would be in the same mood and that in future the former would not cause anyone to miss the train.'

'Bradshaw' (1870) listed five weekday trains each way between Chester and Denbigh. Additionally, a train left Mold at 8.5am, calling at all stations to Denbigh, arriving there at 8.54am. On Saturday night a departure left Mold at 9.30pm, calling at all stations to Hope, returning to Mold at 10pm.

The new line gave improvedcommunication between Denbigh and Chester, the journey saving 11 miles over the previous 41 mile route from Denbigh to Chester via Rhyl.

In 1879 both the Mold branch and the M&DJ were to suffer appalling disruption and structural damage. The M&DJ Board minutes give little away concerning the events of 16th-17th August that year when the area suffered the worst rainfall in living memory. Continuous rain led to widespread flooding, property damage, crop destruction, halting of mining, and severe curtailment of railway services throughout North Wales. The most notable railway incidents, as a consequence of the weekend's deluge, was the destruction of the Llandulas viaduct near Abergele and the derailment of the Irish Mail at Caerwys. Both events had severe repercussions for the passage of important mails and passengers between London and Dublin via the steam packet ships at Holyhead.

The storm began at noon on Saturday 16th August and rain continued to fall without break for almost 30 hours until the early evening of Sunday. One eye-witness described the storm as being of 'tropical intensity'. The effect of so much precipitation was to see the Clwydian and Halkyn mountain ranges release millions of gallons of rainwater in torrents down normally quiet streams.

The raging water in turn pushed up the levels of the River Dee together with the smaller Clwyd, Alyn and Wheeler rivers.

Throughout Saturday night and into Sunday water levels rose rapidly. The River Dee burst its banks at Mostyn, submerging the C&H main line. Several railway bridges in the Denbigh area were washed away or damaged and in places flooding rose to a height of five feet above rail level. On the C&H main line, the Sunday down day Irish Mail reached the floods at Mostyn and owing to the depth of water, the train was forced to return to Chester. The Irish Mail then set out over the Mold branch in an attempt to reach Holyhead via Denbigh and Rhyl. In torrential rain, near Caerwys, the locomotive's weight distorted the rails of the waterlogged track and the engine rolled over. The driver escaped injury although the fireman broke his ankle; only one passenger was injured. The marooned passengers were given shelter at nearby inns. Others were taken to Maesmwynan Hall, Caerwys. Word was still to reach these luckless Irish Mail travellers that the now-abandoned train would have got no further than Rhyl that Sunday, owing to Llandulas viaduct being swept away during the afternoon. A relief train, from Denbigh, got no further than Bodfari. The great depth of water and the dangerous state of the permanent way prevented any further progress. Much of the track ballast had been washed away. Later that night, the connecting steamer 'Ulster' sailed empty from Holyhead for Kingstown, her passengers and mail from the derailed Irish Mail having failed to reach the port. The type of locomotive involved in this derailment of the Irish Mail is not known, but in the late 1870s, locomotives of the 2-2-2 'Lady of the Lake' class, stationed at Stafford, were responsible for working the Irish Mails between Euston and Holyhead.

Monday dawned with sunshine but Chester station was busy receiving urgent telegrams seeking urgent assistance with the destruction wrought by the severe weather. A Denbigh telegram reported that the M&DJ was blocked in both directions three quarters of a mile from Caerwys with river debris eight feet high. Traffic between Caerwys and Bodfari was being worked by lorries [sic]. The down line was reported blocked between Bodfari and Mold and Denbigh Junction with only a single line in operation; Clwyd Bridge (between Denbigh and Bodfari) was 'giving way'.

A further telegram from Denbigh said:

'Bridge over the Clwyd between

here and Bodfari has commenced giving way; unsafe for all traffic.'

Hope station sent a telegram giving news that:

'Both lines at Llong are still under water, and in a very bad state. Nothing can be yet done to them.'

From Mold a telegram stated:

'The waters at Rhydymwyn are down but are still three feet deep. The bridge and roads at Alyn siding are damaged, and will not be ready for traffic for some time. Passengers from Chester on this line cannot get beyond Padeswood. The Irish Mail is embedded about three miles from Mold.'

Contemporary newspaper reports of the flooding in the Chester Chronicle gave detailed coverage of the damage caused. It appeared that only the Vale of Clwyd line remained operational throughout the deluge. Remarkably, no fatalities had occured throughout the weekend flooding. A 'special correspondent' for the Chester Chronicle who visited Mold on the Monday (after completing his journey from Chester in a horse and trap from Padeswood station) reported that:

'Mold Railway Station had a death-like quietness. Not a person was to be seen, the rails were yellow with rust, and the usual appearances of life in the goods yard and offices had disappeared.'

People from 'the hill districts', he wrote, had turned up at Mold station that Monday morning intending to go by a cheap excursion train to Manchester and much to their chagrin were turned away and left to wander the streets. The Alyn Tinplate Works was 'considerably damaged' with the sidings rendered useless. The nearby bridge over the River Alyn (as reported in the Mold telegram) had its supporting masonry washed away by the raging torrent; only the girders and rails remained, suspended in mid-air. At Nannerch the correspondent reported that 'an immense amount of debris had gathered' with piles of rubble covering the railway for over 200 yards, with one mound reaching the arch of the station's road overbridge.

As the waters receded throughout Monday, workmen were extracting new ballast from disused pits near Padeswood station, in order to quickly restore the trackwork but it was Tuesday, 19th August before the first train was able to leave Mold at 12.30pm for Chester. All services between Mold and Denbigh were suspended until 25th August when single line operation came into use, full services resuming on 15th September.

An unidentified LNWR 'DX' 0-6-0 stands in Bodfari station with a train for Denbigh. The coaches appear to be six-wheelers with a first class only vehicle on the right. The village of Bodfari, with St Stephen's church, stands on the hill. Ray Davies Collection.

Chapter Four
Traffic Results and an Eminent Departure

Despite the optimism of the promoters, traffic grew only slowly over the M&DJ, for the line merely connected two small market towns, and further expansion was hampered by the unwillingness of the LNWR (who ran the trains) to make the most of the line's potential. To gauge some idea of the traffic performance, the M&DJ's minute books show that passenger traffic gave the highest number of receipts, closely followed by minerals, then merchandise and finally livestock.

These recipts were often affected by climate, season, disease.and trade depression. In 1872 the M&DJ minutes record:

'The unprecedented wetness of the season. Some of the lead mines in the neighbourhood were stopped, in consequence of the works being overpowered by the water; this not only affected the traffic going off the line, but diminished the consumption of coal.'

Mineral traffic peaked in 1887 having contributed one third of the total MDJR traffic receipts; this had slumped to one fifth by 1903, no doubt reflected by the growing difficulties in lead mining and com petition from American and Australian ores.

Livestock traffic was mainly seasonal, being concentrated in the autumn when cattle, in large numbers, moved out of Wales into England. An outbreak of foot and mouth disease in the spring of 1883 caused all traffic, with the exception of minerals, to decline. Passenger bookings throughout that year were badly affected owing to the necessary cancellation or curtailment of cattle fairs and markets

Trade depressions towards the end of the 19th century also saw a general reduction in business for the M&DJ. Trade was locally depressed in 1876, 1879 and 1881. The years 1885, 1893 and 1895 widened trade depression to national proportions and this too was mirrored in M&DJ receipts. The minutes, more often than once, noted:

'Decline in traffic unfortunately requires no explanation, being due to the same causes which have affected railways over the whole country.'

But there were bright spots. In 1876 an extra 9,000 passenger journeys were made over the M&DJ in connection with the Art Treasures Exhibition and National Eisteddford, held at Wrexham that year. By 1900 passenger receipts made up 60% of the total M&DJ revenue. The military could also provide a temporary boost to the financial figures, as in August 1909, when20soldiers of the Lancashire Territorial Force camped at Caerwys, the M&DJ minutes remarking that:

'The character of the ground renders the locality very suitable for army training and sham fighting.'

One cannot help thinking that the beauty of this part of Wales would give no hint to these very same soldiers of the devastating trench warfare which lay just a few short years ahead.

If the Mold branch should ever have had a regular, distinguished user then that person must have been William Ewart Gladstone, four times prime minister of Great Britain. Although Gladstone was of Scottish descent, the Gladstone family seat lay at Hawarden Castle, a short distance from the Mold branch at Broughton. Gladstone is best remembered, in railway circles, for the introduction of what became known as 'Parliamentary trains'. These measures arose in his Railway Act of 1844 while Gladstone served as President at the Board of Trade. This Act compelled railway companies to cater for the poorest of the community. Each company, which derived a third or more of their receipts from passenger traffic,was to provide a passenger train over every line each weekday. Parliamentary trains were to call at all stations with a fare not exceeding one penny per mile. In addition, the train was not to travel at less than 12mph between stations.

Throughout his long political life, Parliamentary duties at Westminster and political campaigning elsewhere would have seen him come and go through the gates of Broughton and later Broughton Hall station without comment, although he once remarked that on his journeyings, the LNWR looked after him very well. Perhaps the most visible sign of this was a substantial brick-built waiting shelter on the up platform at Broughton. Not even for Gladstone, who often insisted on travelling third class, the dubious weather qualities of a standard Crewe-built wooden hut!

Much publicity surrounded his death from cancer at Hawarden in May 1898. Gladstone had already left public life and had retired to Hawarden but news of his death spread rapidly. Although he had fallen from favour with the monarchy, the poor and less well-priviledged, for whom he and his wife had done so much, took to the streets in great numbers on the day of his private funeral service at Hawarden Church. From the church, the coffin, borne on a bier in turn by parties of colliers, labourers, estate workers and tenants, was taken through the village and park to Broughton Hall station. At the station, where hundreds had gathered to pay their last respects, a special train awaited Gladstone's 'final departure' for London.

Let 'The Graphic' give a contemporary account of the funeral procession at Broughton Hall station:

'At Broughton Hall station, where the railway line cuts the road by a level crossing, the throng reached its summit in numbers. The mounted police and the soldiery could scarce thrust back the solid block along the road so that the railway gates could be barred across it; and the furthermost limits of the throng were hidden by the clouds of dust of late-coming arrivals from Chester. The neighbouring fields were nearly full, and the hedges were breaking down under the pressure put upon them. The train had been long in waiting at the platform. It was a train specially caparisoned, and it was drawn by an engine which thirty-two years ago was named after the great man whom it was now to draw to his burial-place. The railway officials, with a graceful, albeit a rather curious sense of appropriatness, had painted the engine black. The van which was to hold the body was hung with violet and silver. The entraining of the coffin was the work of a very few minutes; it was wheeled up the platform and gently lifted into the mortuary carriage. Mr Herbert Gladstone and Mr Henry Gladstone said goodbye to Mrs Gladstone, the doors were shut, and the carriages drove away. As the train began to glide slowly out of the station, a cry was raised 'hats off', to which the black, stolid North = 20 Country crowd responded as one man, and Hawarden and all that pertained to it was left behind. It was nearly eight-o'clock and growing dusk.'

Perhaps the eye witness for 'The Graphic' was unfamiliar with the livery of LNWR locomotives; there was nothing coincidental about No. 1521 'Gladstone', a 'Precedent' 2-4-0 being painted black. Since 1873 all LNWR locomotives had been painted 'blackberry black' and a beautiful shade of black at that!. However, an eye-witness LNWR driver recalled that No.1521 had been specially prepared and painted for Gladstones's funeral train, the locomotive wearing a shade of paint known at Crewe as 'dead drop black'.

Slowly departing from Broughton Hall, Gladstone's funeral train was seen by an unbroken throng of people, young and old, for the first three miles of the journey into Chester. At Mold Junction engine shed, drivers and firemen jumped down from their locomotives to stand to attention; signalmen and other railway staff did likewise, some saluting in military fashion. Chester station was crowded with people, hats at their side to watch Gladstone's final passing. Such scenes were to be repeated at most stations on the journey south, the train running non-stop in the gathering darkness until reaching Willesden in north London. Here an engine-change took place before20the funeral train continued into central London via Kensington and the District Railway to Westminster Bridge station.

Ex-LNWR Webb 5ft 6in 2-4-2T 6611 outside Denbigh shed. Nine of these secondary and branch passenger tank engines were allocated to Denbigh in 1937. Crewe Works built 160 of them between 1890 and 1997.

Chapter Five
LNWR locomotives - and Omnibuses

In 1905 the LNWR initiated the first motor bus services in North Wales. A batch of Milnes-Daimler double-deck vehicles of London design and seating 34 passengers began public services linking Mold with Flint and Connah's Quay as from 10th July 1905. Further services commenced on 2nd April 1906, linking Mold with Holywell via Halkyn. In 1912 a bus garage was opened at Mold opposite the station buildings. These pioneer bus services continued to run, with many route alterations, up to the First World War. The LNWR had no powers to operate buses but in 1909 the position was legalised by Sections 16 & 17 of the LNWR Act (1909) which gave powers to the LNWR to provide road vehicles and convey mails on them. In the First World War the Army requisitioned the vehicles and shipped them over to France to help in taking soldiers to the trenches. Many, like their uniformed passengers, were destined never to return and few ever took up their

original peacetime duties. Motor bus services would not resume on a large scale until the early 1920s but prior to the First World War, the LNWR had already laid the foundations for future road versus rail competition in Flintshire.

As described in the first chapter, the earliest locomotives used on the Mold branch were Trevithick 'Crewe Type' engines but other than this scant fact, information, records and photographs concerning locomotive matters on the Mold line are scarce – though No.247 'Mammoth', a Trevithick 'Crewe Goods' 2-4-0 in tank engine form is noted as being for use on the line. In that event it was no doubt stationed at Mold. But there were other engines. One was 'Heron', a small firebox 2-2-2 built in 1852. All could not have been well with its performance on the Mold Branch. A LNWR Executive Committee minute of 7th August 1856 recorded complaints made against 'Heron' and ordered it replaced by a better engine. Ramsbottom's Crewe-built 'DX' and

'Special DX' 0-6-0s designed for both freight and passenger work succeeded the early 'Crewe Types' on the Mold line. By 1900 Denbigh engine shed, first opened in the 1860s, hosted about twenty engines, mainly Webb 5ft 6in 2-4-2Ts and Coal Tanks, together with 0-6-0s. Denbigh and Chester sheds shared the passenger turns and the latter would have provided 'Precedent' and 'Jumbo' 2 4 0s.

On 1st October 1890, Mold Junction shed opened, primarily for freight work in the Chester area. The new shed and accompanying marshalling yard were able to take some of the pressure off the LNWR's 'Top Shed' at Chester, situated alongside the Chester to Crewe line. As a direct consequence of the new facilities at Mold Junction, the small shed at Mold closed, to become a grain store. By 9th November 1912 Mold Junction (coded 37 by the LNWR) had 32 locomotives on its books. The complement was made up of a 4 cylinder compound 4-6-0 of the 'Bill

A LNWR postcard view of a Milnes-Daimler double deck bus. Seating 34, this early type of public vehicle, powered by a 24hp Daimler petrol engine through a constant mesh gearbox, was quite a trend-setter and they saw reliable and widespread use by railway companies prior to World War One. Most were requisitioned by the Army and shipped to France to assist in the war effort. One early recruit to railway bus driving was George Edward Parry of Llong. George drove this vehicle and also took the fares. He retired as porter/signalman at Llong in 1953 after 47 years of railway service. The Milnes-Daimler was garaged at Mold station and had a speed limit of 12 mph.

Bailey' 1400 class, three 'DX' 0-6-0s, four 4 cylinder 0-8-0s of the 'B' Class, one 4 cylinder compound 2-8-0 of the 'E' Class, twelve 17in 'Coal' 0-6-0s, seven 0-6-2 'Coal Tanks' (coal side tanks), one 0-6-0 'Saddle Tank Coal' and three 0-6-0 'Special Tanks.' These locomotives reflected Mold Junction's heavy freight, shunting and pick-up duties. Longer distance freight turns from the marshalling yard took engines and their crews to Holyhead, Crewe, Manchester, Birkenhead, and Liverpool.

With so many railway staff engaged in work at Mold Junction, the LNWR provided two streets of company houses on the north or Saltney Ferry side of the C&H main line. These were known as Ewart Street and North Street, reached via the Saltney Lane overbridge. In addition, a 'barracks' was opened for overnight accommodation of railwaymen. To generations of railwaymen however, Mold Junction will always be known by its nickname of 'Spike Island' on account of the iron railings surrounding the houses. In 1920 Mold Junction was host to several war-surplus ex-Railway Operating Division 2 8 0s. A very large dump of these redundant engines – no fewer than 198 – had been established at nearby Queensferry, awaiting buyers.

By 1927, with Mold Junction now under LMS ownership, eight ex-ROD 2-8-0s were allocated but by 1932 only three, Nos.9460, 9462 and 9464 remained and all had been withdrawn by 1933. Despite their pleasing Great Central Railway design, these locomotives, built initially for hauling munitions and troops in France, were unpopular on the LMS. Contemporary reports suggested that the locomotives were kept in deplorable condition but doubtless they proved capable engines for working heavier freight trains over Kinnerton bank. Ten years after the scrapping of these second-hand ROD 2-8-0s, history was to repeat itself with the appearance at Mold Junction of a new type of wartime 2-8-0 whose design and building lay on the other side of the Atlantic.

Top. **Kinnerton station on 30 June 1959, looking in the down direction at the foot of the 1 in 43 Kinnerton bank. Among lush green fields that typify the English and Welsh border country in this area, the station served the villages of Higher Kinnerton and Lower Kinnerton. Standard LNWR wooden huts suffice at the station, although the wooden platforms have been replaced in concrete since opening in 1897. By 1959 the goods yard, which was behind the buildings on the left, had been closed and lifted. Concrete sleepers lie on the up platform, ready for the engineers to begin permanent way renewals. As late as 1962 this wayside station was rumoured to stock LNWR tickets – 40 years after the LNWR ceased to exist! Photograph Mowat Collection.**

Bottom. **'MM' 2-8-0 2394 about to pass under Hoole Road bridge at Chester General station about 1922. Several of these engines, purchased new by the L&NWR from the Government at the end of World War One, were allocated to Mold Junction. Enginemen referred to them as 'Military Marys' although the official name 'MM' was derived from 'Ministry of Munitions'.**

A summer evening view of Denbigh shed, taken on 6 July 1935 with a Class 4F 0-6-0 rubbing shoulders with an ex-LNWR 2-4-2T. In 1937 Denbigh housed nine Webb 2-4-2Ts, one MR 2P 4-4-0 and an L&Y 0-6-0. Under the 1933 LMS 'Motive Power Area Locomotive Supply, Repair, Concentration & Garage Scheme' this twin-road building was categorised as a 'Garage Depot' along with Holyhead, Bangor and Rhyl, the 'Concentration Depot' being Llandudno Junction where periodic examinations and repairs to all engines in the '7' district took place. The late J.M. Dunn of Llandudno Junction and later Bangor fame, was appointed Running Shift Foreman at Denbigh in 1938 but the move was cancelled when the existing RSF refused promotion. Photograph Author's Collection.

Chapter Six
Developments and Dissatisfaction at Denbigh

The LNWR, ever mindful of its shareholders, was often reluctant to improve its rural lines and Denbigh station provides a prime instance. Despite enlargement in 1885, trains, arriving from three different directions, still jostled for a space alongside the station's sole through and single bay platform. A passenger unfamiliar with Denbigh's operating practices would express alarm as the train, on the down loop line, 'missed' the station before coming to a halt and then reversed into the through platform to the rear of a train already occupying the same track. Aggrieved by the possible danger of backing in passenger trains and the meagreness of one and a half platforms, which it considered quite unbefitting to the town's 'county' status, the Town Council complained to the Board of Trade in 1907. Col H.A. Yorke for the BoT visited the town on 30th August that year and reported that 'this method of working is objectionable and might in the absence of special care lead to an accident'. He advised an end to it 'as soon as possible'. In response, the LNWR had plans for a separate down platform, linked by footbridge to an extended up platform but nothing was done and the station remained unaltered until closure.

Perhaps Euston's priorities lay elsewhere for 1906 saw their 'Denbigh Curve' Bill passed by Parliament. This link, commencing between Bodfari and Trefnant, would have permitted direct running from Mold to Rhyl and avoid reversal at Denbigh. However, inertia seems to have crept in and the Act's powers were allowed to lapse, much to the relief of Denbigh's Town Council who feared a loss of trade should the town be by-passed.

Dismayed by Euston's abandonment of their 'Denbigh Curve', the M&DJ succeeded in Parliament with their own 'Bodfari Curve' Bill of 1914. This gave powers for a similar double track line of 1 mile 4 chains at a cost of £18,876. Unfortunately the First World War intervened and the curve was never completed. However, the 1914 Act also gave powers for the purchase of land for a new halt, to be known as Star Crossing, between Rhydymwyn and Nannerch. This was in response to repeated pleas to the LNWR (who characteristically did nothing) by prominent local residents for a halt to serve the villages of Cilcain and Rhes-y-cae. The new stopping place, which took its name from a nearby public house on the Denbigh road, opened on 2nd November 1914. According to the *Flintshire Observer*, it was anticipated that Star Crossing would lead to the development of Cilcain as a holiday resort, the district being popular (to this day) with people from Liverpool, Chester and other parts. The optimism proved short-lived for Star Crossing, together with Llong station, closed on 1st January 1917 as a wartime economy measure, although both reopened in 1919.

Despite having no direct access to Rhyl, the M&DJ in the 1890s did carry seaside excursion traffic from the neighbouring WM&CQR, which had running powers over the line via the south to west Penyffordd curve. These excursions from Wrexham were composed of ageing (by 1900) ex-LNWR four-wheel coaches. The late J.M. Dunn, in his published history of the WM&CQ (Oakwood Press) portrays the decrepitude of these vehicles by relating an amusing incident near Caerwys where a roof lamp fell into the lap of a worthy Caergrwle butcher, decanting rape oil all over his best attire. The company by way of compensation could do little to alleviate his shock and distress, but they did buy him a new suit!

Although the LNWR served over a dozen collieries in the Mold and Coed

A pair of cyclists on the road north from Denbigh to Trefnant give no attention to a Webb 2-4-2T passing over the bridge just north of Denbigh at Plas Clough on August 11 1920. Note the early road sign.

Official portrait, taken in 1877, by the Gloucester Wagon Company Works photographer, of No.11, a simple covered planked wagon with hinged roof and side doors and equipped with dumb buffers and wooden brake blocks. Despite its simplicity, the Glan-yr-Afon Lime Co. wagon probably had a longer working life than its sophisticated 1960s successors, the twin silo pressure discharge 'Prestwin' wagons which predominated in the sidings at Rhydymwyn for but a few brief years.

LNW Webb 2-4-2T 2219 stands outside Denbigh shed on 17 September 1919.

A busy scene at the north end of Denbigh station, 20 June 1920. A Rhyl train stands on the left while the train on the right appears to have a horsebox attached to the rear. Today it is hard to comprehend the sheer volume of traffic carried by the railways before the widespread use of motor vehicles. D.S. Ffoulkes Roberts.

Denbigh station in LMS days, looking south towards Ruthin. The loop line over which trains arriving from Mold would pass if another train occupied the through platform is in the centre of the picture. Denbigh No.2 signalbox is behind and above the gabled building on the left. An ex-LNWR two coach set stands in the Rhyl bay platform. The attractive goods shed can be seen behind the water column. There are further sidings, for coal traffic, on the left. Author's collection.

Talon areas in the years leading up to the First World War, coal traffic had begun a steady decline. Much of the coal mined served only local needs for the North Wales coalfield lacked an adjacent deep-water port for exports. Oil imports, competition from the bigger South Wales coalfields and flooding forced the closure of many Flintshire collieries and despite the temporary re-opening of some pits, by the 1930s colliery traffic had ceased.

At Rhyd-y-goleu, just west of Mold on the Denbigh road, the Alyn Tinplate Works was established in 1874 on the site of a cotton mill. Although on a modest scale, it thrived for many years, becoming a subsidiary of Richard Thomas & Co. Ltd until closure in 1939. For the last two years of World War Two the Ministry of Supply took over the closed works as a storage depot but in 1946 it was dismantled. Even after closure the works name was perpetuated on the signal box responsible for the sidings. These were resuscitated to serve the present-day Synthite works where chemical production started in October 1950 on the former tinplate site. In the earliest days of Synthite, the company owned an Andrew Barclay-built 0 4 0ST named 'Alynva'. Constructed in 1922 and bearing works No.1761 on her builder's plate, 'Alynva' was scrapped in January 1951 and replaced by an even older locomotive with an interesting and varied history. This was 'No.3', a four-wheeled petrol-driven locomotive built by the Motor Rail and Tram Car Ltd of Bedford (Simplex was the trade name)

and supplied new to the Lancashire and Yorkshire Railway at Horwich in 1920. It bore works No.2033. From Horwich the diminutive locomotive was transferred to Merseyside for use inside goods depots, working first at Sandhills and later at Edge Hill. Withdrawn by the LMS in November 1930, the Simplex was sold to the Barnstone Cement Co. Ltd in March 1931, based at Waltham-on-the-Wolds, Leicestershire. This location closed in 1941 and once again the Simplex found itself under new owners, namely R. Robinson and Co. Ltd, a firm of contractors. After probable use by the contractors at a number of locations, 'No.3' was bought by Synthite Ltd in 1950 and after a further life of fifteen years was finally scrapped in 1965, to be replaced, like its predecessor, by an even older locomotive!

Further private siding traffic was concentrated mainly at Hendre, near Rhydymwyn where limestone quarrying and lead mining had been carried out for decades. Lead was mined by various companies with up to nine shafts sunk but by 1908 they had been abandoned after flooding. The opening, in sections, of the 10ft wide Milwr Drainage Tunnel which eventually stretched for eight miles from its outlet at Bagillt (on the River Dee) to beneath Rhydymwyn station brought about a revival in lead extraction. A 1ft 10in gauge railway, built for construction of the tunnel, was retained and although not having direct connection with the standard gauge Mold-Denbigh railway was responsible for the extraction of lead

and movement of stored ammunition during World War Two. A fleet of battery-electric and diesel locomotives which eventually totalled ten was used. The most profitable output from the Milwr tunnel turned out to be water itself, used by Courtaulds at their man-made fibre factories at Greenfield near Holywell Junction, on the Chester to Holyhead main line. Other sidings at Hendre served the Ruby Brick and Tile Works while Dolfechlas Crossing and Hendre Sidings signalboxes controlled access from the up side of the Mold to Denbigh railway. Regular limestone trains left Rhydymwyn for Pilkingtons at St Helens. A quarry at Gwernymynndd near Mold also generated limestone for Lever Brothers at Port Sunlight. Used in their calcining plant, it was carried in three-plank, dropside 'half-box wagons', possibly lettered L.B. Ltd; this traffic was brought by lorry to Mold. At Rhydymwyn the North Hendre Lead Mining Company used 'Gwen', an Andrew Barclay 0 4 0ST, for internal shunting. In 1902 The British Portland Cement Co opened a siding at Caerwys although their own works was situated some distance from the railway. In 1921 the Partington Iron & Steel Company began limestone quarrying at Bodfari. The quarry was used for the extraction and crushing of 'haematic' limestone. At the quarry's peak of production, 150 workers were employed. The limestone, for use in the company's blast furnaces at Irlam, Lancashire, was transported from the quarry face by an internal railway which made connection with LMS metals via

GWEN, an Andrew Barclay 0-4-0 saddle tank built in 1900, poses outside its shed at the Halkyn & Hendre Lime Co's Works at Rhydymwyn. Photograph H.W. Robinson Collection, Industrial Railway Society.

the goods yard at Bodfari, located on the up side of the Mold-Denbigh line. The Irlam company brought 'Arkayar', an 1880-built Hudswell Clark 0 4 0ST from Irlam, to work at Bodfari. The sidings, connecting the quarry to the goods yard opened on 14th August 1923.

Outgoing limestone was loaded into Partington's own high-sided 20 ton open wagons. Incoming tank wagons brought tar for mixing with lesser grades of limestone for the production of tarmacadam. Some of the tarmac produced was of poor quality due to a fall of soil from the hill behind the crushing plant but the most noteworthy feature of the quarrying at Bodfari were the clouds of red dust which settled on the houses in the village. In 1930 the Partington Iron and Steel Company was taken over by the Lancashire Steel Corporation which in 1932 closed down the Bodfari operation. The exact fate of 'Arkayar' is unknown but it is thought to have been scrapped before the take-over. In 1951, the quarry sidings were briefly re-opened for use by A.D.H Pennant but by 1960 the rails had been removed.

Above. ARKAYAR, a Hudswell Clark-built 0-4-0 saddle tank built in 1888, draws wagons over the road into Partington Iron & Steel Co's sidings behind Bodfari station in 1929. The first wagon is lettered PARTINGTON BODFARI while the second appears to be an oil tank wagon. Photograph R.G. Pratt Collection, Industrial Railway Society.

Below. LNWR six-wheel, 30ft stock stands in the through platform at Denbigh, September 17 1919.

Webb 2-4-2T approaching Blue Hand Bridge with an up train to Chester on September 12 1921. Behind the rear of the train are the earthworks of the abandoned 'Bodfari Curve' which would have enabled trains from Mold to run direct to Rhyl over the Vale of Clwyd branch, thus avoiding Denbigh. Photograph D.S. Foulkes-Roberts.

A Chester train departs from Denbigh on 20 June 1920 past Denbigh No.1, a 38 lever frame signal box which survived until the resignalling scheme of 1956. The sidings adjacent to the signal box dealt with cattle and general merchandise. The wagons on the right are standing on what was known as the Ruthin siding. Photograph D.S. Foulkes-Roberts.

A 1959 view of the rarely photographed Star Crossing Halt, between Rhydymwyn and Nannerch, looking west. The original wooden platforms have been rebuilt in concrete in the same manner as at Kinnerton. The weather-beaten standard 'Crewe' hut on the up platform is still in the LMS colours of light stone and dark brown. Photograph Mowat Collection.

With steam to spare, Webb 5ft 6in 2-4-2T 6624 brings an up Denbigh to Chester six-coach semi-fast through Kinnerton, c1930. The engine carries a front number plate, a fitting that did not last long on ex-LNWR engines. The entire train is in LMS livery, but completely LNWR in origin.

Broughton & Bretton's LMS-built signal box, photographed from the shelter of the down platform in BR days. The level crossing gates are open to road traffic on the main A55 Chester to Bangor via Hawarden road. Today the new A55 'North Wales Expressway' cuts through the trackbed of the erstwhile Mold branch approximately a mile further south. The up combined home and distant signal protects the level crossing but the lower signal arm is controlled by Mold Junction No.3 signal box.

Chapter Seven
Heady Days Between the Wars

Amost notable event in the history of the Chester to Denbigh line took place on 16th July 1920 when the LNWR royal train, conveying King George V, Queen Mary and their daughter Princess Mary, arrived at Denbigh for the Royal opening of the nearby Llangwfan Hospital. The train travelled from Holyhead via the Vale of Clwyd branch and also carried senior LNWR officials including Chief Mechanical Engineer C.J. Bowen-Cooke. While the royal party visited Llangwfan Hospital, the train was stabled to the south of Denbigh station, on the single track line to Ruthin. After the royal visit, the train proceeded over the M&DJ and although not booked to stop at Mold, by prior arrangement slowed appreciably for the townsfolk, gathered in a field near the tinplate works.

In 1922, the LNWR ran ten passenger trains each way, with variations between Chester and Denbigh. Three continued to Corwen, the entire 48 mile journey taking 2 hr 50 min, including a pause of 20 minutes at Denbigh to change engines. The first up departure of the day from Denbigh, the 6.28 am to Chester, offered a London connection; after arrival at Chester at 8.8 am, passengers could await the

arrival of the 7.35 from Birkenhead Woodside which conveyed through carriages to London Euston with an arrival in the capital at 12.10 pm. The return journey would be made from Euston at 5.20 pm with a Chester arrival at 9.1 pm. A short walk to Platform 1 would find the 9.25 pm for Denbigh waiting. An additional four trains ran each way between Mold and Denbigh; only these workings (at that time) served Star Crossing Halt. At Hope Exchange, connections for Wrexham were more favourable than those to Seacombe but the underlying thought is that both the LNWR and the GCR paid scant regard for each other's timetables, exemplified by the 5.47 pm arrival from Denbigh coinciding with the 5.47 departure for Seacombe!

On 19th March 1923, the board of the Mold & Denbigh Junction Railway held their last meeting following the company's absorption by the newly-formed London, Midland & Scottish Railway as part of the grouping of most of Britain's railways into four big companies. The M&DJ had survived as an independent railway company for 62 years and following loss of office, the outgoing Company Secretary, Mr H. Milner Willis, Mr A. Hay, Traffic Agent

and Mr H.A. Sanders, Solicitor each received compensatory sums of £600, £400 and £500 respectively. The Company's final bank balance stood at £5,042 10s 2d, (equivalent to the sum of £139,627 at 1989 prices). So ended the life of a small railway company that owned neither locomotives or rolling stock but had, through its determination to link Mold with Denbigh, given Euston more than a few management headaches.

The 1923 amalgamation into the 'Big Four' railway companies effected little change, outwardly, in North Wales. Throughout the 1920s ex-LNWR Webb tank locomotives continued to thrash their way through to Denbigh, with only the company crest and initials and the engine number altered, to those of the LMS. Yet external pressures began to materialise. For the first time the Chester to Denbigh line faced a degree of road competition, for in 1921 omnibus services in the district recommenced after the wartime break with the Crosville Motor Company, based at Chester, opening a Chester to Mold service that year. The following year a Mold to Denbigh service was inaugurated, the Crosville vehicles operating almost in parallel with the

A mainstay of branch passenger services at Denbigh for almost 50 years, Webb 5ft 6in 2-4-2T 6669 takes a rest by the water tank in LMS days. The fireman looks as if he is trying to escape the ergonomic vagaries of the cab. It is claimed that Francis Webb designed engines like these with the sole purpose of taking the skin off the knuckles of engine crews!

Caerwys on April 24 1936; 'George the Fifth' class 4-4-0 5343 OTTERHOUND is lifted by the Crewe 36 ton steam crane to enable a fresh pair of driving wheels to be substituted. The engine was put in the down siding after the trailing couple axle broke while it was pulling away from Caerwys with a passenger train for Chester on April 13 that year. The 'get-you-home' repair was carried out with the help of the Llandudno Junction breakdown gang and the locomotive was safely returned to Crewe Works for withdrawal and scrapping. Of background interest is the very tall L&NWR home signal post at Caerwys station. The height was essential for sighting purposes, for behind the photographer was a road overbridge which partially obscured the approach to the station.

trains, on the adjacent coach road. Crosville, soon to become a household name throughout North Wales, Cheshire and Merseyside, expanded their services throughout the 1920s and most outlying villages in the Mold and Denbigh area eventually came to be served by omnibuses.

The success of the omnibus services did not gone unnoticed by the LMS who, from 1st May 1929 bought Crosville out and for a period of one year, various saloons (the Crosville term for a single deck vehicle) and double deckers appeared with the branding 'LMS Crosville' on the maroon and cream bodysides. Euston decided to keep the goodwill of the name Crosville, no doubt respecting any misgivings by die-hard busmen about being taken over by a railway company. Thus for the second time in twenty years omnibuses carried railway insignia in Flintshire and Denbighshire.

A year later the LMS sold half its shareholding to the Tilling and British Automobile Traction Ltd and the new company became known as Crosville Motor Services Ltd with the LMS still retaining three directors on the board. A 'Road and Rail Standing Joint Committee' was set up with the aim of promoting and combining road and rail travel. Buses and trains would connect at stations. There would be prior notification between each company of proposed timetable changes, there

would be inter-availabilty arrangements of return tickets, reciprocal advertising and combined parcels services. An example of a bus connecting with a train at a railway station was the acquisition by Crosville, in July 1930, of the firm W. Edwards of Denbigh, whose vehicles plied the mile distance between Caerwys station and the town.

The preceding paragraphs serve to illustrate that, contrary to some belief, 1930s bus and rail companies were not always locked in ruthless competition for business, particularly in rural areas, Indeed much additional revenue was generated by the inter-availability of road and rail tickets.

The daily routine of timetabled goods and passenger workings was often interspersed by annual events. One such event was the Chamber of Trade outing. In 1934 members of Mold Chamber of Trade and the Rhydymwyn branch of the Women's Institute combined forces for an excursion to London. The bright lights of the capital were the choice once again in 1935. The subsequent local press report, written by a correspondent with an apparent eye for technical detail, provides a valuable insight into how the LMS spared no effort (for Chamber of Trade members were valuable customers of the railways) in organising special workings. An extract follows: *'There must have been a great whirring of alarm clocks in Mold and district on Thursday morning! - and I can bear*

testimony to the efficiency of one of them. The platform was black with people at 7 o'clock that grey, serene September morning and all the stragglers had arrived by 7.15 when the long train steamed in from Denbigh. There were seven passenger saloons, two kitchen cars, and an extra piece of rolling stock known technically, I believe as a 'compo-brake.' The train was again in charge of Mr C. W. Ricketts (on behalf of Mr P. Kinsman, Goods and Passenger Superintendent at Chester). With Mr Ricketts in charge you just 'take your place with the party,' and everything 'just happens' as arranged. The passengers numbered 287 plus one Press representative who was the happy guest both of the LMS Railway Company and the Chamber of Trade. The train staff (including cooks, dining car attendants, etc) numbered about 15. Within a minute or two of the scheduled time the special train steamed off on its long journey, while the land was still covered with the mist of Autumn morning.'

Under the LMS, passenger services were much improved and 1938 saw a peak of fifteen weekday departures from Chester to Mold, Denbigh and beyond. Late on Saturday nights, two further trains departed from Chester at 11 and 11.48 p.m, for the benefit of cinema-goers, calling at all stations to Denbigh. Sunday trains, a feature of the line's earliest days, also reappeared in the summer months, between July and September. In the hot summer of 1934 four out and back workings ran between

Webb 2-4-2T 6629 rounds the curve at Chester on the approach to the elevated No.6 box. The locomotive heads a down train for Denbigh, formed of six-wheelers. The photograph appears to have been taken shortly after the 1923 grouping, for the coaches are in LMS crimson red livery. A freight is passing in the up direction while a LNWR 4-4-0 takes water on the left.

Chester and Denbigh during the afternoon and evening, an excursion fare from Chester to Denbigh costing 3/9d. Perhaps sleepy Star Crossing Halt was not quite ready for Sunday trains, for in the early hours of Sunday, 6th July 1934, the last down passenger train of the previous day, running an hour late, smashed into the level crossing gates (left open for road traffic) and reduced them to matchwood. After bringing their train to an emergency stop, the engine crew jumped down from the footplate to search for anyone who might be injured but luckily found no-one hurt and quickly resumed their late running journey! The beginning of World War Two saw a drastic curtailment of services and the late night and summer Sunday trains disappeared from the timetable for good.

A US Army Transportation Corps S160 2-8-0, built by Lima and shipped to the UK in 1942. The LMS were loaned fifty of these locomotives and after certain detail modifications for home use, they appeared at Mold Junction for a few months before further shipment to the Continent after D Day. In total some 400 were loaned to the 'Big Four' companies.

Webb 2-4-2T 6627 has steam to spare as it approaches Bodfari with a Chester-Denbigh train. Although the photograph is dated 26 May 1939, the scene is pure LNWR. Only the replacement concrete fence posts could claim to be LMS. Photograph E.R. Morten.

Ancient and modern at Denbigh in 1938. An almost new Stanier 2-6-4T 2483 buffers up to an elderly ex-LNWR Webb 2-4-2T in the bay platform at the north end of the station, 5 June 1938.

Broughton and Bretton station on 1 July 1959. The signalman has already accepted a train from the Mold direction and the level crossing gates have been closed to road traffic on the busy A55 Chester to Hawarden road. The LMS-style signalbox replaced an earlier one first opened in 1877. The main station building is of Francis Thompson design and very similar to his design for wayside stations on the Chester and Holyhead main line. The substantial hipped-roof waiting shelter on the opposite platform is noteworthy. Broughton station was very close to Hawarden Castle, family seat of the Gladstone family. It would be safe to assume that W.E. Gladstone himself used this station at the beginning of his journeys to Westminster. In turn, the LNWR would have been anxious to provide him with somewhat superior accommodation to that of the station wooden 'Crewe' hut! Photograph Mowat Collection.

Special freight duty 'Black Five' 4-6-0 45001 draws out of the goods yard at Mold with an export consignment of Jones baling machines which were produced at Mold during the 1950s and 1960s. The 1950s were a time of 'export or die' for British Industry as the UK tried to reduce its foreign debt following the near-bankruptcy of the nation after World War Two. The very tidy appearance of the permanent way (it was all done by hand) is worthy of note. A figure can be seen crouching on the lofty L&NWR bracket signal, under the lower arm, which signalled traffic onto the Coed Talon branch, over the crossover in the foreground. 45001 was a Mold Junction engine for much of the 1950s and lasted almost to the end of steam. Her final shed was Carnforth and withdrawal came in March 1968, with eventual scrapping that year at Drapers of Hull. Photograph Glyn Morris.

On 14 December 1938 work proceeds on the installation of the first set of points and crossover leading to the site, on the left of the Vickers Armstrong Factory, then under construction. The photographer is facing north-east with Broughton & Bretton goods yard on the right-hand side, behind the stationary engineers' train. BAE Systems.

Chapter Eight
Wartime Events and Evacuees

The coming of war in Europe and on the high seas brought about a great increase in traffic, particularly between Rhydymwyn and Mold Junction. On Friday, 1st September 1939, the LMS, in a well-executed plan, organised special evacuation trains from Merseyside. These brought English evacuee children from the Liverpool, Wallasey and Birkenhead areas into towns and villages in North Wales. Mold received approximately 450 children of school age and they were given a warm welcome by townsfolk who were to take them into their homes. After the first weekend of war some children returned home, unused, after a mere 48 hours, to the idea of a quieter and safer life in the country. With no immediate prospect of German bombing, the 'phoney war' as it became known, encouraged many parents to have their children returned home. They would have remained quite safe in familiar surroundings until the ferocity of German attacks on Merseyside in the latter part of 1940 drove Merseyside children back into North Wales.

Adjacent to Broughton & Bretton station, Messrs Vickers Armstrong opened a huge 'shadow' factory in 1939 for the production of the famous twin-engined Vickers Wellington bomber. The assembly lines employed over 6,000 people, many of them women, at the peak of wartime production. The Broughton site was chosen not only for its good rail and road links with the rest of Britain but also as a means of reducing local unemployment. In the Mold district alone, over a third of registered workpeople had been jobless in 1938.

To supply the factory with building materials and aircraft component parts, work began in January 1939 on laying sidings into the site from the up line north of Broughton and Bretton station. A John Fowler 40hp 0-4-0 diesel mechanical locomotive (Works No.22753) was supplied for shunting wagons within the factory area. A similar 40hp John Fowler locomotive arrived, second-hand, in 1945; Works No.21999, it served at Broughton for only three years, before being sold to the Barrow Steel Co Ltd in 1948.

Later in the war four-engined Avro Lancaster bombers, built under sub-contract, supplemented the Wellingtons on the production lines. Over 5,000 Wellingtons had been produced at Broughton but as World War Two ended, demand for warplanes rapidly declined and the factory's future appeared in doubt. But as the last aircraft left the factory, to be test flown and then scrapped as unwanted, Vickers turned the plant over to producing aluminium pre-fabricated houses to meet the urgent need for new and replacement housing throughout Britain. Popularly known as 'prefabs', a weekly output of 170 units was built up from 1945 until 1948. Unfortunately Vickers apparently favoured road transport rather than rail for the supply of these houses. Contemporary photographs show completed prefab sections being transported from the factory by articulated low-loader lorries.

In contrast to Broughton's visible (and audible) end products, the establishment, also in 1939, of a large Royal Ordnance chemical factory complex at Rhydymwyn was done in great secrecy. This site, tucked away in the narrow Alyn Valley and no doubt chosen for its remoteness from enemy action, produced munitions including the filling of shells with mustard gas. The poison gas was brought in by rail

Workmen struggle with the waterlogged ground at Broughton – a feature of this low-lying area – as preliminary drainage work begins on the Vickers Armstrong aircraft factory, 1939.

An empty Denbigh shed, long since vacated by locomotives but otherwise still intact when photographed on 28 May 1961. In 1989 the shed still survived as a road haulage depot, the surrounding area being developed as a small trading estate. Photograph W.T. Stubbs Collection.

On 7 August 1948, Compound 4-4-0 1098 halts at Hope & Penyfford station with the 2.25pm Corwen-Denbigh-Chester train. In that year Chester (LM) shed had an allocation of 16 of these Midland Railway-derived locomotives for main line and secondary passenger work.

Railway and construction site staff pose with Mold Junction 4F 0-6-0 4073 on 20 January 1939, before the locomotive ventured on to the newly completed Broughton aircraft factory reception sidings. The site official is standing on the track leading to what became the 'Goods Inwards Dept.' of the Vickers factory. Broughton and Bretton station stands behind the wagons on the left. In 1991 the track still remained in situ at the Broughton Factory, now owned by British Aerospace.

Standing water still hinders progress on the initial drainage work at the site of the new Broughton aircraft factory, 4 March 1939.

The rebuilt Denbigh shed in 1952, three years before closure. Outside stands 2P 4-4-0 40396. After the Midland merged with the London & North Western in the 1923 'Big Four' grouping of companies such engines as these become widespread throughout former LNWR strongholds in North Wales. They were ideal, but dated engines, for secondary passenger and branch line work. Alongside is Ivatt 2-6-2T 41224 built at Crewe in 1948 and destined to finish its working life at Bournemouth in June 1967. Equipped for pull/push working 41224 was the modern equivalent of 40396 in terms of capabilities. Denbigh was coded 38D in LNWR days but by the 1920s had declined in importance and in the LMS era become simply a sub-shed of Rhyl, coded 7D. Of interest is the white painted wall of the wooden hut, used to monitor coal stocks. The siding to the right led to a 42ft turntable. Until the turn of the century this had been located at the north end of Denbigh station.

from ICI's chemical plant at Runcorn. In 1942 Imperial Chemical Industries started work (code-named 'Tube Alloys') at Rhydymwyn on a model plant for the separation of uranium by gaseous diffusion, in connection with work on the atomic bomb. Approximately 2,400 workers (a direct bus service from Rhyl brought in many Royal Ordnance employees who lodged in the numerous boarding houses and hotels in the town) were employed in several large camouflaged buildings, linked by an extensive internal railway system; connection with the down Denbigh line was made half a mile south of Rhydymwyn station. To cope with the increase in freight traffic generated by the Rhydymwyn factory, the LMS provided a new signalbox (equipped with a 45 lever frame) and signals in 1940. Prior to the signalbox opening, traffic at Rhydmwyn had been controlled by a 6 lever station ground frame.

For shunting and marshalling wagons over the sharp curves within the factory, two small locomotives, one steam, one diesel, were drafted in by the Ministry of Supply. Andrew Barclay supplied an outside cylinder 0-4-0 saddle tank, No.8, Works No.2095. This powerful locomotive, equipped with 3ft 7in driving wheels and 16 x 24 in cylinders, was new on 11th November 1940. In

April 1949 No.8 was sold to the ICI Wiggs Works at Runcorn and a decade later passed to the Britannia Scrap Metal Co. Ltd of Widnes. Preceding the delivery of the steam locomotive, an 80hp 0-4-0 diesel-mechanical shunter, No. 5 built by John Fowler (Works No 22906) and also supplied new, arrived in September 1940 and was to serve at Rhydymwyn for almost two decades.

For many years after the war the factory, known as the 'Valley Works', was omitted from Ordnance Survey maps. Gas-filled shells produced in the factory were stored in numerous old lead mine workings adjacent to or beneath the factory area but how much of it was actually produced remains unknown. Local lore has it that part of a research 'Tube Alloys' nuclear trigger device was transported away from the factory in a hearse! In wartime Britain few people were prepared to openly ask questions about anything that happened at Rhydymwyn and many events went unreported. The German High Command was well aware that something went on at Rhydymwyn, for references were made to it in propaganda broadcasts, but they were unable to locate the factory complex, so well was it camouflaged. Even today an air of mystery surrounds the remaining buildings of the factory

complex which are still Government owned and now used for storage.

The idea of being remote from enemy air attack was rudely shattered on the night of 13th March 1941, when a German aircraft swooped low and machine-gunned a stationary passenger train in Caerwys station. According to the local police station logbook no casualties were reported but for reasons of censorship, no mention of the attack was made in the local press. In an incident the previous year, the Luftwaffe, en route to blitz Liverpool, dropped a stick of high-explosive bombs over the Padeswood area, one bomb falling on the Mold line, disrupting services for a period.

In 1943 the last down train of the day from Chester, the 8.45pm to Denbigh, normally provided a connection out of the 4pm ex-Euston (arrive Chester 8.29pm). However the London train was often heavily delayed and to minimise delays, the 8.45pm departed on time. The LMS then provided a connecting 'ghost train', which ran most nights, stopping as required to set down only, in the blackout, between Chester and Denbigh. At first the coaches remained overnight at Denbigh but after a week the practice was to return the empty train to Chester late on Saturday nights. On one occasion the train lived up to its

Dolfechlas Crossing signal box, a LNWR 'Composite 4' standard structure opened in 1898. Equipped with a 22 lever frame, the box was abolished on 1 January 1969. Photograph I. Vaughan.

Stanier 2-6-4T 42461 stands at the closed Coed Talon station on October 2 1955, during an RCTS tour. Station retains its original angled LNWR booking office sign, seen under the canopy. Photograph T.J. Edgington.

name by returning in the small, dark hours of Sunday morning, rousing rural lineside inhabitants from their beds, for after the passing of the timetabled 8.45pm to Denbigh there was normally no more traffic until early Monday morning. The 'ghost train', usually the preserve of a Chester tender engine, consisted of three coaches. In January 1944 the 8.45pm was retired to depart earlier at 8.35pm, the London train arriving a minute later at 8.36pm!

The 1 in 33 Ffrith branch played no part in the war effort, having being closed and lifted in the spring of 1935 following a derailment on 29th July the previous year. Standard 3F 0-6-0T No.7374 had left Coed Talon for Mold Junction with a train of nineteen mineral wagons, two carrying earthenware pipes. When approaching Pontblyddyn bridge over the Mold-Wrexham road, the driver, to his alarm, noticed the third wagon from the engine jumping over the sleepers. Putting on steam in a desperate attempt to straighten the train before crossing the bridge, only the locomotive and the first two wagons made it, the rest of the train toppling over. A passing motorist looked up in astonishment as at least fourteen wagons rolled down to the foot of the embankment. From the resulting mass of splintered body-work and shattered drain pipes the goods guard emerged unscathed. The poor condition of the

sleepers had led to the rails spreading under the weight of the train and the breakdown train, sent to clear away the wreckage, proved to be the last movement over the line. The coal pits, the *raison d'être* for the line had all been worked out or abandoned due to geological problems by the 1930s and re-instatement of the track was not justified, especially as the LMS could still serve Coed Talon via the Mold (Tryddyn Junction) line. It had opened first as a colliery branch in 1869, a four and a quarter mile line later upgraded for all traffic by the LNWR. A service of four passenger trains each way on weekdays between Mold and Coed Talon commenced on 1st January 1892. In 1898 the passenger service was extended to Brymbo over the LNWR and GWR Wrexham & Minera Joint Railway. Thus, the opportunity arose for the traveller (with time to spare) to travel from Mold to Wrexham and back using three different railway companies- outward by LNWR to Brymbo, there to take a GWR train to Wrexham. After arrival at Wrexham (General), the return journey could be made by boarding a GCR Seacombe-bound train at the adjacent Wrexham (Exchange) station, changing into a down LNWR train at Hope Exchange, and alighting at Mold to complete a round trip of just 24 miles.

Up to and including the early years of World War Two, the Chester to

Denbigh line retained a strong pre-grouping company atmosphere, with Webb 5ft 6in tanks monopolising the passenger workings, supplemented at times by 'George V' and 'Precursor' 4-4-0s displaced elsewhere by new LMS standard types. A unique wartime working was reported in the July 1942 *Railway Observer* when, on 20th July that year, a G1 0-8-0 No 9033 made short work of Kinnerton bank with a three coach Denbigh train. By 1943, trains were reportedly in the hands of Stanier 2-6-4Ts, 2-6-2Ts and 2P 4-4-0s, but the 5ft 6in Webb tanks still managed two or three workings a day, with occasional forays by Coal Tanks.

Following shipment into Birkenhead Docks from America in the summer of 1943, a batch of USA 2-8-0s was allocated to Mold Junction and these machines, with their distinctive American lines must have made a strange contrast with the resident home-grown 0-8-0s. The American engines will be looked at in greater detail in a subsequent chapter dealing with life at Mold Junction engine shed. This shed had one passenger turn in 1943, the Saturdays only 4.15pm Chester to Denbigh, which was hauled by either a 4F 0-6-0 or a Stanier 2-6-0.

The tour train had started at Chester for a run down the Chester and Holyhead main line to Prestatyn, thence up the Dyserth branch (reverse), on to Rhyl, Denbigh, Corwen (reverse), Denbigh and then over the Mold and Denbigh Junction to Mold. From Mold the train traversed the Coed Talon branch (reverse) and then went on to Wrexham Exchange before returning to Chester (Northgate) via the WMCQ.

Participants in the RCTS railtour stretch their legs during a pause at Mold on 2 October 1955 while Stanier 2-6-4T 42461 waits to uncouple and run round the train before returning to Chester, after a visit to the freight-only Coed Talon branch. The tour included the Rhyl-Denbigh-Corwen and Dyserth lines of the former LNWR. The outward journey departed from Chester and reached Rhyl via the Chester & Holyhead main line. Photographs T.J. Edgington.

A view east from the A541 road overbridge showing Nannerch station with not a soul in sight! However, some activity is on the cards as the signals have been pulled off for a Denbigh-bound train. There was no box, the signals being operated from a ground frame on the station platform. A solitary 16 ton steel goods wagon stands in the siding behind the platform, indicating that in July 1959 when this photograph was taken, freight traffic was sparse. The practice of painting the station name in large letters on the main building is unusual. Even in 1959 station lighting at rural stations like these would be by oil lamps with the station name illuminated in small letters on the lamp glass. The cattle dock siding leads off the picture to the left. No trace of this station now exists for the site was cleared to re-align the A541 and eliminate a sharp double bend produced by the road overbridge. However, in 1991 a loading gauge and wooden hut were still visible from the road, serving as a reminder of a more leisurely mode of transport. Photograph Mowat Collection.

Featherweight branch goods; a begrimed 75054, a Mold Junction Standard 4-6-0, brings a solitary 16 ton coal wagon and brake van into Nannerch from the Denbigh direction during the winter of 1961. In 2003 the realigned A541 Mold to Denbigh road occupies the former trackbed at this point and little evidence remains of the railway at Nannerch. Photograph A. Sainty.

Chapter Nine
Accelerating Branch Line Decline

By 1950 all the Webb 2-4-2Ts, with their characteristic Victorian tall chimneys, domes and oft-scorched smokebox doors, so much part of the North Wales branch line setting, had departed either for scrap or further service in the Midlands. A visit by railway enthusiasts to Denbigh shed in March that year revealed a complete absence of LNWR locomotives. Instead the shed roads contained brand new Ivatt 2-6-2Ts Nos.41231 and 41232. Older types were represented by a 2P 4-4-0 No.40671, Compound 4P 4-4-0 No.40925, ex-Lancashire & Yorkshire 2-4-2Ts Nos.50678 and 50687 and, still in LMS livery, ex-Midland Railway 3F 0-6-0 No.3396. It was normal practice to change engines on through Chester to Corwen trains at Denbigh, local crews preferring the 2P or 4Ps with their greater water and coal capacity over the stiff grades of the eighteen mile run down to Corwen.

The abolition of petrol rationing and the growth of private car ownership after World War Two brought about a slow decrease in the use of the area's rail services. The unpunctuality of passenger trains, cited in a 1946 Flintshire County Council report, could have done little to stem this decline. With the railways in state ownership as British Railways following nationalisation in January 1948, a fresh look was undertaken by the Branch Line Committee of the British Transport Commission. It was this committee's brief to assess lines for possible closure. Initial closures undertaken by the newly formed London Midland Region of BR were not long in coming. First to go was the weekdays only Mold-Brymbo branch service of two passenger trains each way which ceased on 27th March 1950. Passenger traffic, even during the war, never warranted anything more than a locomotive and single coach. In 1944 a Mold Junction 4F 0-6-0 reportedly handled the passenger (mainly schoolchildren) workings. Between these trains the locomotive shunted at Mold and worked freights to Brymbo. Three years later on 2nd February 1953, passenger trains were cut back from Corwen to Ruthin, followed by cessation of trains between Denbigh and Rhyl on 19th September 1955, leaving Ruthin as the terminus of through trains from Chester via Mold and Denbigh. However, the line remained open throughout from Rhyl to Corwen for freight and the 'North Wales Land Cruise' summer excursions. The early post-war years also saw the revival of seaside excursion trains from Wrexham to Rhyl via Mold and Denbigh. In the summer of 1952, a six-coach excursion

ran empty from Wrexham to Gwersyllt, there to pick up mining families intent on swopping their grim industrial surroundings for an invigorating day on the seafront at Rhyl, much as their forebears had done from the turn of the century.

Despite the first closures, 1953 proved to be an eventful year on the Chester to Denbigh line. The Queen's coronation at Westminster Abbey was expected to generate considerable extra passenger traffic. In connection with this event the London Midland Region advertised a special excursion to Euston, starting from Ruthin on 1st of June at 9pm (where the return fare would have cost 45 shillings) and calling at all stations to Chester, thence direct, through the night, to London.

The morning of Saturday 15th August that year might have been an early turn the relief signalman at Dofechlas Crossing would have preferred to forget. Having pulled off his signals for the 8.15am Mold to Denbigh which had already departed from Rhydymwyn station, the signalman had to leave his box, descend the steps and manually close the crossing gates to road traffic. A passing lorry, lumbering over the rails, distracted the signalman's attention from the rapidly advancing train. Having lost critical seconds the signalman managed only to push one set of gates clear of the line before having to jump for it into a nearby ditch as the locomotive crashed into the remaining gates, smashing them to pieces and damaging related safety equipment. Services were delayed for a short while as the splintered baulks of white-painted timber were cleared to one side.

At the Valley Works, Rhydymwyn, the wartime stockpiles of mustard gas shells began to be disposed of. Much of it was destined to be taken away and dumped at specially allotted seabed sites in the Irish Sea. Signalman Ron Mills who started his railway career at Mold in 1938 remembered on some occasions opening Rhydymwyn box at 4am in order to allow special workings of freight trains carrying the poison gas to leave the Valley Works sidings. 'The Rhydymwyn box, opposite the factory, was a heavy frame to work,' he recalled, 'and the special trains with their deadly cargo left early in the morning so as not to attract any attention. They kept it all very quiet.'

Wartime had seen heavy use of the rail network and by the early 1950s much overdue renewal of worn out trackwork was underway. The complex set of crossings and points in the area of Chester General station became due for replacement in late 1953. Ninety pairs of points and no fewer than 170 sets of

diamond crossings were renewed; much of the new trackwork was prefabricated at Mold during the week before transfer to Chester for installation over the weekend.

On the debit side, the two-road engine shed at Denbigh, rebuilt as recently as 1948/49, closed from 19th September 1955 upon the withdrawal of Rhyl to Denbigh passenger trains. The small complement of Ivatt Class 2, Fowler and Stanier 2-6-2Ts were transferred out of the district, leaving solitary Midland 3F 0-6-0 No.43396 to soldier on from Rhyl shed, which assumed responsibility for the remaining freight turns to Denbigh, Ruthin and Corwen. Chester took over all passenger workings and in September 1956 a batch of Standard Class 4MT 2-6-4Ts arrived for local passenger work. These almost new engines, with their well-appointed cabs, must have been a godsend to engine crews who until so recently had put up with the dubious comforts of the elderly Webb tank engines.

By 1956 the total of down passenger trains had dropped to nine, but these were supplemented by unadvertised early morning workmen's trains. One left Denbigh at 6.15am for Mold, while from Chester a return working served Broughton & Bretton for the benefit of workers at the now De Havilland-owned aircraft factory. The intermediate Mold-Denbigh service had dwindled to one late afternoon return working, while on Saturdays (rather wastefully) empty coaching stock ran from Denbigh to Mold to form the 12.55pm all stations to Denbigh, presumably for the benefit of afternoon shoppers.

In January that year the line saw its first diesel multiple unit, a Derby Lightweight, making a trial run. With a Lancashire driver at the controls and accompanied by a Mold Junction pilotman, the green twin car unit excited great interest upon reaching Ruthin. Points raised in the press at the time noted the diesel's lightweight construction, seating for 130 and greater economy and flexibility in use. The new train pointed the way forward to a brighter, cleaner future for local rail travel but there was a cloud on the horizon that very day. Signalmen on duty noted that the dmu, powered by adapted bus engines, lost time on the steep 1 in 43 Kinnerton bank. This fact did not go unnoticed by railway management; they would, in later years, use the excuse that contemporary dmus were not powerful enough to climb the bank. This was presented as an argument for *not* modernising the Chester to Ruthin passenger service, sealing its fate.

An early 1960s view from the north end of Denbigh station, showing the 1957 signal box and the revised signalling. A pair of passenger coaches (right) lie over awaiting their next turn of duty while box vans (right) suggest that Denbigh goods she was dealing with a healthy level of general merchandise. Such traffic was to thrive (and increase) along the Vale of Clwyd branch from Rhyl long after passenger traffic had ceased to Rhyl and Chester.

In 1962 the signalman at Denbigh hands the fireman of a Chester-bound train the single line token for the Denbigh to Bodfari section. The train has left the bay platform, once used by departures to Rhyl. BR Standard Class 4MT 4-6-0 75028 and a Stanier 2-6-4T rest between duties. Photograph G. Harrop.

Chapter Ten
Life Aboard the Pick-up Goods

Goods traffic in 1956 consisted of one early morning Mold Junction to Denbigh through working followed by an all stations pick-up turn, shunting en route as required. Several freights continued to serve Mold and Hope Junction together with a daily working to Coed Talon. Coal supplies from Wrexham to Connah's Quay power station was worked via Hope Junction and the west facing curve at Mold Junction. Hendre Sidings, Rhydymwyn was also served, with an arrival at 12.56pm from Mold Junction, shunting as requested at Broughton & Bretton, Kinnerton Siding, Hope Junction, Padeswood & Buckley and Mold. Up loose-coupled trains were allowed five minutes at a stop board to pin down wagon brakes before descending Kinnerton bank with a further five minute pause at Broughton & Bretton to pick up brakes.

The daily routine of pick-up freights in the 1950s had its lighter moments. Owen J. Hughes, then a Fireman based at Mold Junction, recalls an episode that left the Guard of one such train ashen-faced as he stood on the platform at Bodfari with the tail lamps of his brake van quickly receding under the bridge:

'We arrived at Bodfari with the 8.35am Denbigh to Mold Junction stopping freight. We were a few minutes early with our short train. The wagon next to the engine was to be taken off. The Guard uncoupled and pinned down the brake of the second wagon. Within a few minutes we were back again with our train having placed the loaded wagon in the yard. Our Guard quickly coupled up and 'picked up' the brake on the second wagon. It was at that moment that the Stationmaster arrived, no doubt to take particulars of labels off the wagon and have a deep conversation with the Guard. At this point a little information about our Guard would help complete the picture. Jack Thomas, a short, portly man, had been Secretary of the National Union of Railwaymen, Mold Junction Branch, for years. He was also associated with various functions at Saltney Ferry and was well-liked. He was a stickler for Rules and Regulations and Union matters and with a fair knowledge of politics was in great demand everywhere.

'Realising that we could be another five minutes or so before departure I crossed the footplate and sat on the seat. The type of locomotive we had was a Class 4F 0-6-0, an ex-LMS standard type with left hand drive, which was very convenient for the driver with all the shunting and signals on his side. Suddenly my driver said "Jack must be in", meaning getting aboard his brakevan, "because the Stationmaster's disappeared behind the wagon".

'We were both of the opinion that we had missed him getting into his van. So with the starter signal in the 'clear' position at the end of the Bodfari platform and with no more ado my mate opened the regulator and away we went, next stop Caerwys some two miles further up the line. My mate settled in on his seat, situated on the reversing gear high up in the cab corner, filling his pipe with tobacco, while I put a few shovelfuls around the firebox. With the resultant smoke trailing down the left side of running, we carried on, blissfully unaware of the drama that was soon to unfold...

'Suddenly my mate said "There's somebody waving to us here!" I crossed the footplate to look. A narrow road ran parallel with the railway at this point and I could see a huge motorcycle which I had seen earlier adjacent to the station house at Bodfari. I immediately opened the steam jet to disperse the smoke and give us both a clearer view and to our amazement I recognised our Guard on the pillion, white-faced, hanging on like grim death and

BR Standard Class 4MT 4-6-0 75010 draws into Rhydymwyn station on a wet Saturday, April 21 1962.

Above and below. The scenic delights of the Chester-Denbigh railway. A BR Standard Class 2 2-6-0 heads the 12.49 SO Chester to Denbigh in winter sunshine on 25 November 1961, at the Blue Hand Bridge between Bodfari and Denbigh. The church at Bodfari can be seen in the middle distance, overshadowed by the Clwydian range of hills. Photograph Norman Jones.

Denbigh station, at the north or Rhyl end of the main platform, in 1959, 4F 0-6-0 in the bay. In the middle stands the new BR Denbigh signal box. Opened in 1957 and containing 70 levers it was to have a working life of only nine years, closure taking place on 19 June 1966. The top half of the signal box and the lever frame were recovered and re-erected at Oxley, Wolverhampton. The sidings on the right had a capacity of 124 wagons. Photograph Mowat Collection.

Denbigh station in 1959 with a Mold Junction Stanier 2-6-0 heading a two or three coach Chester train in the through 'up and down' platform. The left-hand line is the loop line, over which down passenger trains passed through (when the platform was already partly occupied) before halting and then reversing into Denbigh station. Beyond the junction home signals, in the background, the line continued as single track, southwards to Ruthin and Corwen. In the late 1950s Mold Junction shed assumed some responsibility for passenger turns to Denbigh and beyond to Ruthin. This 2-6-0, one of nine allocated to Mold Junction at that time, would have forged its way up Kinnerton bank with little trouble. Photograph Mowat Collection.

clutching his shunting pole. Little wonder for it was no way for a man in his sixties to travel at the speed that was necessary to catch us up.

'Instantly we realised the whole situation. My mate brought the train to a stand at a convenient spot nearest the adjoining road but with a little stream running between. Jack, not a candidate for athletic pursuits, eventually reached our engine but not before he had collected a shoe full of water en route. No word was said as he made his way to his van but if looks could kill we'd have been six foot under. On seeing Jack safely aboard, the Stationmaster (a keen motorcycle enthusiast) turned and headed back to Bodfari.

'My mate and I during conversation on the matter couldn't understand why Jack hadn't put the handbrake on in his van at Bodfari as per normal practice which would have prevented us from leaving. Perhaps his trust in us was greater due to the fact that we were both members of his union. Heaven forbid had we arrived at Caerwys without a Guard. Natural progression for such an act would have involved officialdom and a pretty stink that would have made.

'We arrived at Caerwys, conscious of the brake being applied by the Guard and in such a cute way that the train came to a

stand on a tight coupling, resulting in my mate having to reverse each time to uncouple. We were indeed, as they say in the grade, eating humble pie.

'Eight weeks later came the same turn of duty with the same team and the first opportunity to talk about that incident. We were at Denbigh and with time permitting, we ate our sandwiches together in the brake van. This opportunity for a chat made an enjoyable week. On this particular day Jack asked beforehand if I could bring him some oil. Once we had settled into the van Jack confided that he needed the oil to lubricate the handbrake. At last the incident was well and truly on the agenda. Amid laughter Jack said, "Only for the motorbike I'd have had to walk to Caerwys", to which my mate replied, "Never mind Jack we would have waited for you!"

'I think we laughed loudest because we had seen something Jack hadn't – the look on his face as he rode pillion passenger. As far as we knew Jack Thomas never again left his brake van without first applying the handbrake. Our own personal view was that the Bodfari incident was simply a one-off thing.'

The Coed Talon branch from Mold was also host to an amusing incident which in this case the engine crew did not only lose the Guard but the brake van as well!' Owen J. Hughes described what happened: 'On one occasion we left Mold for Coed Talon with engine and brake van, the latter being propelled and as was customary any parcels for Coed Talon were put in the brake van. We set off, picking up the staff for the single line branch at Tryddyn Junction Signal Box. Our four mile journey was uphill most of the way and on reaching the highest point of the journey, the line would go downhill into a dip, pass under an overbridge and disappear where the line curved and then rose steadily into the platform at Coed Talon. Our Guard for the week was Doug. We had come to know him very well although he hadn't been at Mold Junction for long; he had spent some time in the police force and originally came from Manchester. On reaching the summit my mate closed the regulator, to free-wheel into Coed Talon. To our amazement, upon looking out, there was no sign of the brake van! Obviously it could have only gone one way, forwards to Coed Talon. It must have sped like a bullet to disappear so quickly round the corner by the bridge, a fair distance from the summit.

The early 1960s saw a rapid increase in passenger services 'axed' by BR, in a vain attempt to reduce mounting financial losses. Each final day of services brought about a formal ritual often bordering on the macabre. On their own initiative, local staff would ensure a specially cleaned locomotive, complete with small headboard or wreath. Enthusiasts and opponents of the closure would often turn up wearing top hats and black armbands. A mock coffin may well have made an appearance. No such ritual was apparent (or allowed?) in this view of the 8.50pm Chester to Ruthin. It appears to be business as usual in Platform 1 at Chester General. Can it really be true that Standard Class 4 4-6-0 75033 awaits the guard's whistle for the very last down departure for Mold, Denbigh and Ruthin, on Saturday evening, 28 April 1962. Photograph Brian Cowlishaw.

'As I had personally hooked on with the engine shackle, there was no way that the van had become loose by accident. We were a little apprehensive as we turned the corner only to find that the brake van had come safely to a stand near the station buildings and only yards away from the crossing gates which were permanently left open for road traffic. Our Guard was already busily unloading parcels off the van. The Porter/Shunter at Coed Talon, who had witnessed the incident, said he couldn't believe his eyes when the solitary brake van came into view round the corner. He said laughingly, "I didn't know what to do. My first impulse was to look around for traffic on the road. I thought there might be a danger of the brake van crashing through the gates but as it came near I realised that the Guard had complete control over his van. He worked the handbrake very well!"'

Wagonload traffic to and from Rhydymwyn's Royal Ordnance factory had ceased by 1960 with the track lifted that year; prior to this and apart from special workings, a daily down pick-up freight sufficed for any custom. The resident John Fowler 80hp 0 4 0 diesel mechanical locomotive was transferred away to the Royal Ordnance Factory depot at Chelford in Cheshire and reportedly ended its days, in 1964, at Brackley in Northamptonshire as scrap.

The very last up train to call at Hope & Penyffordd station; Fairburn 2-6-4T 42209 of Chester about to depart with the 7.30pm Ruthin to Chester (General) on 28 April 1962. Behind the footbridge the wartime ARP type signalbox is visible. A Crosville coach is passing over the level crossing. Photograph Michael Mensing.

King Street road overbridge at Mold station about 1959. The original road ran at ground level where the crossover is, prior to the extension of the railway to Denbigh. Behind the covered footbridge is the shed formerly used to house railway omnibuses and lorries.

The former engine shed at Mold in April 1959. Abandoned for locomotive purposes in 1890, the building was adapted for use as a grain warehouse. The smaller extension (right) contained stables. This structure, along with the goods shed and main station building, survived until 1988. Photograph C.A. Appleton.

Mold station, looking east, on a fine day in June 1959. No hint of closure is evident but rumours would already be on the lips of station staff. As befitting a station serving the county town of Flintshire, it appears tidy and well maintained. The platforms and footbridge are well protected from the elements (the LNWR carried out much station improvement work at Mold in 1900) and suspended beneath the canopies ex-LNWR wooden station signs can be discerned. BR vitreous enamel 'hot dog' signs bring things up to date. Beneath the footbridge are various timetable and travel posters; one gives details of excursions to Liverpool and Douglas, Isle of Man. Such holiday destinations were heavily advertised in North Wales. In the distance a WD 2-8-0 is about to draw out of the goods yard and run through the station. A dozen or so of these wartime locomotives were allocated to Mold Junction in 1959. Photograph Mowat Collection.

Chapter Eleven
False Optimism

At the enquiry into the withdrawal of Rhyl-Denbigh local trains, BR gave a solemn assurance that there would be no further branch line closures in the foreseeable future. But concerned Denbigh councillors knew that it would only be a question of time. In 1957 BR stated that the Chester-Denbigh-Ruthin service was secure and 'scheduled for diesel operation'. Further cause for optimism was the commissioning that year of a brand new signal box at Denbigh to replace the three older ones, together with revisions to the track layout, with track-circuiting, between Denbigh and Mold &Denbigh Junction. The latter was abolished and the track singled from Bodfari to Denbigh. Thus, from Denbigh northwards, the parallel Rhyl and Mold tracks were worked as separate single lines, each under electric token. Despite this, the promised diesel multiple units never materialised and passengers remained steam-hauled in non-corridor carriages until closure.

The summer of 1958 brought the first permanent station closures to the Chester-Denbigh line. Padeswood & Buckley (Buckley was over a mile from the station) closed its doors to passengers as from 6th May; freight facilities had been withdrawn earlier on 6th August 1956. At the end of the summer, the lightly-used exchange platforms at Hope High and Hope Low Levels (Hope Exchange until 7th November 1953) closed to little apparent protest with Flintshire County Council raising no objection and the British Transport Commission stating that 'following the introduction of road passenger services the use of the station had progressively declined and the cost of retaining the stations was not justified'.

In February 1960, the motive power situation underwent a subtle change. The BR 2-6-4Ts were exchanged for a batch of the similar LMS-built Fairburn design from Glasgow and these engines, together with Stanier 2-6-4Ts, Standard 4MT 4-6-0s and 2MT 2-6-0s, handled the remaining passenger turns to Denbigh and Ruthin. The late 1950s saw revenue from BR passenger services rising, but at the end of the decade a mild recession hit the country. Freight revenue had suffered a drop and in 1958 the railways recorded a working deficit of £48.1 million, a considerable amount of money in those days. The Government began

sit up and take notice of the year-by-year accelerating losses.

The British Transport Commission, charged with the overall management of Britain's railways since nationalisation, had to be seen to be doing something about stemming the haemorrhage of railway revenue. Despite this, the BTC seemed to have little idea where the money was being lost. Rather than grasping the nettle by reducing its own monolithic bureaucracy, cutting non-essential staff and streamlining railway operating practices, the BTC chose the easy option of closing branch and secondary main lines. Railwaymen affected by these closures would simply transfer elsewhere so staffing costs continued to rise with inflation. Many of these now closed rural railways could have survived if only they had been allowed by the BTC to undergo conversion from expensive-to-operate steam-hauled stopping trains to diesel multiple unit operation, with unstaffed halts. Passenger revenue could have been increased by up to a third. This the BTC knew only too well with branch lines already converted to diesel operation. As it was, the savings over the years

Mold & Tryddyn Junction signalbox, a Saxby & Farmer structure, controlled both the level crossing at Gas Lane and the trailing connection (equipped with spring points) with the Coed Talon branch, curving away to the right, on the outskirts of Mold. This view was taken on the penultimate Saturday of through services to Denbigh, 21 April 1962. Photograph G. Harrop.

from branch line closures were minimal, compared to continual operating losses throughout the 1960s.

Not only were the diesel units cheaper to operate but the clean, bright interiors and panoramic views obtained were a godsend to marketing new train services. The travelling public, who had perhaps endured for far too long the dirt and dinginess of steam-hauled coaching stock, flocked back, with enthusiasm to the new trains, but for passengers on the Chester, Denbigh and Ruthin line the opportunity was not allowed to happen.

The alarm bells of possible railway closures in North Wales were sounded in early 1959 in statements to the local press by Mr F. H. Fisher, District Traffic Superintendent at Chester. Mr Fisher, on the eve of his retirement, predicted complete closure of all the London Midland Region's North Wales lines over a period of ten years with the exception of the important Chester and Holyhead route. The statements attracted considerable comment and criticism particularly from representatives in the tourist trade anxious about repercussions from the resultant lack of rail access to the Snowdonia National Park. Although no wholesale closures were proposed 'for the present', few observers were convinced that the proposals would not eventually go ahead. Newspaper comment, by way of response, put it that British Railways should take a positive role and expand

and popularise existing railway services, in particular the lengthy but highly scenic Conway Valley branch.

Hard on the heels of Mr Fisher's predictions came rumours of possible withdrawal of the Chester-Ruthin passenger trains. This was but one of thirteen passenger services to be considered by the London Midland Region for closure 'during the course of the year'. The LMR alleged that the Chester-Ruthin service was losing £80,000 a year although the true figure according to protesters was thought to be half that amount. Nothing was done to reduce losses by further singling of the track, introducing diesel multiple units to popularise rail travel (dmus were going into service in large numbers on neighbouring lines) or revising the timetable to suit changed needs. Railwaymen knew also that a deliberate 'freeze' on permanent way maintenance was being conducted. Throughout north-east Wales, among railwaymen and passengers alike, it was felt that the line was being deliberately run-down.

Formal notice of closure came in late 1960 with proposed total abandonment of the line between Rhydymwyn (Hendre Sidings) and Denbigh. The unadvertised workmen's trains would continue from Chester to Broughton & Bretton (for the aircraft factory) while Mold, Denbigh and Ruthin stations would remain open for parcels and freight traffic. Opponents of closure formed themselves into the Denbigh

Rail Users Association and local authorities added their weight against closure at a series of meetings in Mold, Denbigh and at the Transport Users Consultative Committee for Wales and Monmouth inquiry held at Ruthin in November 1961. Despite strong opposition to BR's closure plans, a local farmer stood up at one meeting and boasted that the service was so poorly patronised that he could accommodate all the passengers in his car! As a body supposedly representing the interests of the travelling public, the TUCC seldom opposed the closure of branch lines and many protesters suspected that the TUCC had little power or the will to reverse closure proposals. Like many other railway closures the precise financial position of the Chester to Ruthin service was never made public. The TUCC merely confined itself to hearing cases of personal hardship once the passenger trains had come off, never to return. Protesters were shocked to discover that the LMR 1961 summer timetable showed the Chester-Denbigh-Ruthin line as 'Service Withdrawn'. However an addendum stated that the service would continue for the duration of the summer timetable with a supplement listing the train services at the back of the timetable! This was clearly a stratagem by the authorities to discourage any travel at all over the line and so 'prove' the case for closure.

The local newspapers gave plenty of space to the story of impending closure.

Fireman Cleve Jones leans out of the cab of Mold Junction's Stanier 8F 2-8-0 48655 at Mold, after traversing the Coed Talon branch about 1963. Jason, the Mold station porter, adds his smile (right). Cleve remarked that nobody seemed to know Jason's surname! 48655 had been taken to Coed Talon to pick up vans of bagged silica for use in producing 'Vim' by Lever Bros. at Port Sunlight. 48655 moved first to Chester and then to Buxton after Mold Junction shed closed and the 8F was withdrawn at Buxton in August 1967. Photograph Cleveland Jones Collection.

Chester allocated Black 5 4-6-0 45044 lies on its side over a set of vandalised points at Mold Synthite works on October 21 1966. The engine and its train of Prestwin silo wagons were travelling to Rhydymwyn when the accident happened. 45044 was found to be little damaged upon recovery by the Chester breakdown gang. Replacement diesels were already arriving in the Chester district and repairs to 45044 were deemed unnecessary and the unlucky engine was withdrawn.

A survey by the *Chester Chronicle* revealed that on one day, only 468 passengers used the line (the combined population of Mold, Denbigh and Ruthin amounted to 18,455 according to the 1961 census), and the protests and counter proposals by way of letters to the local press and railway management were to no avail. The TUCC report recommended closure of the Chester to Ruthin service to the Central Transport Consultative Committee. In turn the report landed on the desk of the then Minister of Transport, Ernest Marples. The Minister (of road-building fame) duly gave his consent for closure which was to take place as from 30th April 1962.

On Sunday, 22nd October 1961, to mark the impending demise of much of the ex-LNWR branch line network in north-east Wales, the Midlands area of the Stephenson Locomotive Society ran a well-filled six-car dmu excursion from Chester to Corwen via Mold and Coed Talon, before returning to Chester via Rhyl and the Dyserth branch. This train may well be the only time a dmu travelled (in public service) over the Mold-Denbigh section, as well as being the last passenger train to reach Corwen from Denbigh. Much to the delight of the many visiting enthusiasts that day, a wealth of ex-LNWR signals, rolling stock and permanent way were seen. Remarkably, one LNWR distant signal near Mold was to survive a further 24 years until abandonment in 1985.

With only a fortnight to go before closure, a tragic accident took place at Nannerch. On 16th April a newly-wed 22 year-old housewife, attempting to cross the line to meet her husband, was killed by a train. At the subsequent inquest it was revealed that the engine crew, travelling at about 25 mph, had

given adequate warning by whistling at about 200 yards from the crossing. The then Flintshire Coroner, Mr Rhys Llewellyn Jones, remarked that 'The irony of this tragedy is that the railway line has since been closed down.' A verdict of accidental death was given.

Saturday, 28th April 1962 was the final day of passenger services between Chester and Ruthin (there was no Sunday service). On duty at Llong station that day as Porter/Signalman was Mr Harry Loundes of Gwersyllt, Wrexham. Mr Loundes normally worked on the former Great Central Wrexham-Bidston 'Top line' but was also employed as a relief signalman since 1957 at boxes ranging from Mold Junction to Dolfechlas Crossing near Rhydymwyn. He often took the first available train of the day to open up a box. Mr Loundes recalled that traffic over the line was 'routine' and that lime traffic was routed off the Mold and Denbigh section via Denbigh and Rhyl. At some stations, while acting as porter, he recalled that 'you were lucky to take more than twopence' in a day. On the last day, in between operating the signalling, opening and closing the crossing gates and attending to trains, he discovered a 6 x 4in board in the station building. Seemingly forgotten, the dusty board listed the signatures of every railwayman since about 1918 who had worked at Llong. Among them was a note to say that on July 15th 1942, during the darkest days of World War Two, His Majesty King George VI and Queen Elizabeth passed through Llong station at 5.56pm after a morale-boosting tour of factories in Flintshire. Another note recorded the arrival in 1959 of a television crew who had come to film the delivery of the station's domestic water, in cans, by rail. Keen

to see the little board preserved, Mr Loundes, after completing his final shift that Saturday at Llong, took it home – a wise move for the following week a stores train stopped at Llong to enable workmen to strip the station of all booking office equipment, tickets, lamps and nameboards. Anything not required was burnt.

The last down train, the 8.50pm from Chester to Ruthin, headed by Mold Junction's BR 4MT 4-6-0 No.75033 (described in one newspaper report as a Stanier 4-8-0!) left Chester General with no official ceremony or recognition. No time was spared to specially clean the locomotive. The three coaches, however, were filled with well-wishers, regular passengers, and enthusiasts observing and tape-recording the 'last rites'.

At Mold Junction shed a chorus of engine whistles saluted the passing train, while at Denbigh, despite a surprisingly low turnout of only a dozen people, the town's mayor waved off the last up departure for Chester. Mold's platforms were crowded and people lined the road overbridge to give a noisy farewell to the final departure for Denbigh. The mood, according to the *Chester Chronicle* reporter, was hardly one of despondency: 'It was,' he wrote, more like saying good-bye to Aunt Emily: 'Not a bad old stick really, but we can very well do without her!'

Almost every wayside station boasted a throng of people in the oil-light, anxious to witness the final train or take a last ride, and a brisk trade in single tickets from Mold to Rhydymwyn was reported. Sunday dawned with the realisation that in one fell swoop, the county towns of both Flintshire and Denbighshire had lost their railway passenger services. However, much to the LMR's annoyance, the TUCC closure report had recommended the retention of the track between Rhydymwyn and Denbigh for the possible reinstatement of passenger services should the local economy expand. However, the longer the now rusting rails remained throughout the summer of 1962, the greater the feeling of unease at Euston. Railway closures were, and still are, a sensitive subject but this was a Welsh railway closure with all the implications of a decision to axe the line taken by unseen Englishmen in distant London. Fearing that the Flintshire and Denbighshire County Councils would raise the political temperature by calling for the reinstatement of passenger trains the longer the track lay in situ, the order went out from Euston in November 1962 (with the Minister of Transport's approval) to have it pulled up as quickly as possible. The District Civil Engineer at Bangor was instructed to commence lifting from Monday, 17th December that year.

Top left. Mold & Tryddyn Junction. Photographed from the level crossing at Gas Lane in 1959, the 24 level frame structure was the only original box left on the Mold line. The box nameboards differ from the official spelling of this location. The Coed Talon branch curves away to the centre of the picture. The spring points protect the main line from any runaways on the falling grades from Coed Talon. Photograph Mowat Collection.

Left. Participants on the RCTS (Merseyside Branch) Wrexham, Mold & Connah's Quay Railway railtour of Saturday 29 April 1967 gather in the goods yard at Rhydymwyn to watch Stanier 2-6-4Ts 42616 and 42647 run round and couple up for the next part of the tour to Hope Junction and Wrexham, Rhydymwym now being the end of the line. Prestwin silo wagons used for limestone powder traffic from Hendre quarries stand in the yard. On the left are the buildings of the Royal Ordnance Factory, known as Valley Works. Photograph Jim Peden.

Above. The tracklifting contractors arrive at Nannerch; a view from the up platform in 1962. Already the fishplates have been unbolted and thrown onto the platform, to enable the track panels to be lifted by the crane and placed on the bogie bolster wagons left in the station. Such melancholy scenes were commonplace throughout Britain in the 1960s as rural railways were 'axed' in a bid to reign in mounting financial losses on BR. Photograph Lens of Sutton.

The RCTS Wrexham, Mold & Connahs Quay Railtour restarts from its water stop at Mold on 29 April 1967. This view, looking towards Rhydymwn, shows that freight traffic was still abundant at that time. On the left, flat wagons have been loaded with Jones Balers, made in the town, while on the right, general merchandise open wagons await marshalling. Mold signal box, behind the photographer, had been abolished two months previously, the signals becoming 'fixed' distant arms. Freight traffic was withdrawn from Mold in April 1967. Photograph John Goss.

48287 passes over Dolfechlas Crossing, now protected by a sole piece of rope on 5 February 1965. 48287 came to Mold Junction in January 1965 and upon the shed's closure moved to Chester and then to Crewe South where it was withdrawn in June 1967. Photograph Brian Cowlishaw.

Chapter Twelve
Blowtorch and Bulldozer: the Demolition Men Move In

After eight months out of use demolition men carried out their first act of 'surgery', severing for good the single line section west of Bodfari station. Elsewhere on the line, however, things appeared to have undergone little change. Sidings at Mold and Hendre quarries were filled with revenue-earning goods wagons. At Caerwys station on 1st May 1963 it appeared to be business as usual as Mold Junction's 8F 2-8-0 No.48455 rumbled past the weed festooned platforms, heading towards Mold with a brake van. But the tracklifting contractor's gangs, in their quest for material recovery, were not far behind and within weeks there only remained tell-tale depressions in the ballast to indicate where the sleepers had lain. The stations at Bodfari, Caerwys, Nannerch and Star Crossing had their platforms separated by a gravel road. The track was lifted out by crane in 60ft panels and, after inspection by the District Civil Engineer, at least 50% of the rails were found to be fit for re-use elsewhere.

During track-lifting operations the rare occurrence of a wagon running away over four miles was recorded in signalbox registers. A bogie-bolster, loaded with recovered rails from the Nannerch area, rolled away down the grade towards Rhydymwyn, smashing through the crossing gates there and continued, driven by its own laden weight on the falling gradient, towards Mold where the signalman, unable to stop it, alerted his colleague at Tryddyn Junction who then set the points for the errant wagon to be diverted onto the Coed Talon branch. The Tryddyn Junction signalman duly saw it roll past over the junction and up the branch where it came, according to plan, gently to a stop on the rise. Not finished with its runaway exploits, the bogie bolster then rolled back into a refuge siding where the buffer stocks brought any further movement to an abrupt and safe end.

After the completion of track lifting, recovery of signalling equipment and removal of overbridges between Rhydymwyn and Denbigh, the closed station buildings passed into private ownership and remain so today, although Nannerch station was later pulled down for a road improvement scheme. The existing road overbridge which overlooked the station was demolished, thus eliminating a dangerous set of bends on the main A541 Mold to Denbigh road, the realigned road passing through the now levelled former station site. Freight traffic over the remaining Mold Junction to Rhydymwyn section, which for several years remained double-tracked and fully signalled, consisted of domestic coal, agricultural machinery, general merchandise and limestone powder, the latter coming from both Coed Talon and Hendre quarries near Rhydymwyn. However, 1963 brought further closures with the withdrawal on 22nd July of bagged lime powder traffic, in box vans, from Coed Talon, destined for Henry Stoddart's works at Stoke-on-Trent. Closure of Broughton & Bretton station came about upon withdrawal of the workmen's trains on 2nd September. These trains were not without motive power interest for on one occasion the train drew up at Broughton & Bretton with a former Great Western 4700 class 2-8-0 at the head. These nominally express freight engines were employed between Paddington and Birkenhead on overnight goods trains and during the day would be pressed into service on fill-in turns if no other suitable locomotive was available. Ex-Great

48287 propels a raft of hopper and general merchandise wagons into the yard at Hendre Quarry, 5 February 1965. Photograph Brian Cowlishaw.

On a gloomy February afternoon in 1974, an English Electric Class Type 4 climbs the north to west curve to Penyffordd linking the ex-Great Central Wrexham to Bidston line (known locally as the 'Top Line') with the former L&NWR Mold branch. The train, consisting of 'Prestflo' wagons from the nearby Penyffordd cement works, is bound for Coatbridge in Scotland. Photograph Roger Carvell.

Western locomotives, with outside cylinders, did not normally traverse any ex-LMS lines west of Mold Junction due to the risk of their greater width over outside cylinders striking platform edges. Even GW locomotives with inside cylinders were uncommon although one or two did appear on Anglesey and at Llandudno Junction towards the end of regular steam operation on the North Wales coast.

On 21st October 1966 the now truncated Mold line made local news again when 'Black 5, 4-6-0 No.45044, heading towards Rhydymwyn with empty 'Prestwin' silo wagons, was derailed on a set of facing points at the Mold Synthite works, blocking the line for two days. The locomotive left the track and rolled on to its left side, fortunately without injury to the Chester crew. Subsequent investigation revealed that the point blades had been left open by vandals, who had removed a point lever securing chain. The effect had been to divert the left-hand wheels of the engine into the siding. Upon recovery by the Chester breakdown crane, No.45044 appeared to have only suffered minor damage, but repairs were deemed to be not worth while and

the locomotive was condemned as scrap at Chester shed after a working life of thirty years.

Freight trains from Rhyl continued to serve Denbigh and Ruthin via the old Vale of Clwyd branch, changing over to diesel traction in 1967. Ruthin's freight service ceased on 1st March 1965 when local goods facilities were reorganised under the Rhyl Freight Concentration Scheme. This led to the closure of the goods depot at Ruthin despite a direct written plea by the local MP Mr Geraint Morgan to Dr Richard Beeching, Chairman of the British Railways Board. He urged Dr Beeching to reconsider the closure plan, following representations from Ruthin Council. But decisions had already been taken and abandonment had never been a question of 'if' but rather 'when'. The single line of six and three quarter miles was cut back to Denbigh, with Messrs Thomas W. Ward of Sheffield contracted to recover redundant materials.

Denbigh's freight facilities lingered on until 1st January 1968 when closure of all rail operations came about. The cessation of rail freight operations there was bitterly fought against by local authorities, manufacturing firms, coal

merchants, farmers and private individuals who saw BR's LMR headquarters once again 'massaging' its financial statistics in order to prove a case for closure.

Representations were made to the Welsh Office and Parliament. The old Vale of Clwyd line was contributing gross revenue of £100,000 to the London Midland Region and at LM Divisional level the line was known to be viable. To encourage economic growth, Denbigh, in the 1960s, was placed in a development area and on the strength of having an existing rail link, local factories expanded. Goods produced went far and wide. Every month a total of eight long wheelbase continental ferry vans left Denbigh for Ingelheim in West Germany, via the Zeebrugge train ferry, carrying firelighters manufactured by G.E. Platt Ltd. Marsdens Biscuits Ltd had contracts to supply F.W. Woolworth & Co's high street stores and its products were shipped out by railway container on 'Conflat' wagons. Both G.E. Platt and Marsdens Biscuits expected to increase their production and intensify their use of Denbigh's freight yard. Local railwaymen worked hard to provide a reliable service; in 1966 some 36 railway staff were occupied at Denbigh. Inward traffic brought in domestic coal and seasonal sugar beet and fertilisers. To quote the late George Dow, then BR's London Midland Region Divisional Manager at Stoke on Trent with responsibility for North Wales: *'Denbigh is a busy place.'*

In a memo to Euston he argued for the retention of rail facilities at Denbigh and pleaded for operating costs to be adjusted to show how much more economical in branch line operation the recently drafted-in Type 2 Bo-Bo diesels could be. But headquarters at Euston was unmoved by opposition at divisional level. The Denbigh freight branch did not appear on the 1966 Development of British Railways Plan map as a route to be modernised. The Plan pointed the way to fewer, regional freight concentration centres, depots and the use of Liner Trains. The use of continental ferry vans was to be rationalised to permit more intensive use of such vehicles between key centres rather than small towns like Denbigh. The old Vale of Clwyd branch from Rhyl's Foryd Junction to Denbigh, in BR's eyes, had to go. At the risk of existing custom and goodwill being lost to the roads for good, Euston offered Denbigh customers, under the new plan, alternative transhipment facilities at Chester and Mold. Parcels were, in future, to be dealt with at Rhyl. The new freight arrangements proposed by

BR to Denbigh's factories were very much on a 'take it or leave it' basis. BR promised extra lorries to take goods to Chester, once the road overbridge at the closed Bodfari station had been strengthened to take their weight by the LM's District Civil Engineer.

The management of G.E. Platt knew that great care was taken with the loading of their products at Denbigh but suspected that, away from their direct supervision, the larger Chester goods depot would not have had the resources to exercise the same care and attention their firelighters demanded during transhipment from road to rail. Damage to their goods in transit was a risk the company would not take. The firm decided to try out direct road transport to Ingelheim, a fact quickly taken up by the local press.

The policy of opposition by Flintshire County Council to the closure of Denbigh to freight traffic was uneven. The Council, as a whole, was against closure, yet at the same time the subordinate County Surveyor's department was pressing BR for an early date for abandonment of the line. This was in order for their contractors to occupy the trackbed, for construction of the St Asaph bypass which was planned to cross the railway at right angles.

The impending closure of the Vale of Clwyd branch reached the ears of the railway enthusiast world who were ever anxious to travel, in special trains, over

doomed branch lines. The last railtour to visit Denbigh was the LCGB 'Conway Valley' tour which brought specially cleaned 'Crab' 2-6-0 No.42942 and a rake of modern BR Mk1 and 2 coaches under the shadow of the station's cut-down spire (the topmost part had become unsafe) for the first and last time on 24th September 1966. Sadly the distinctive stone-built station buildings, once headquarters of the Vale of Clwyd Railway, were later demolished, although the nearby engine shed remained in use by a road haulage contractor for many years.

Stanier 2-6-4Ts 42616 and 42647 run past Rhydymwyn signalbox on the RCTS Wrexham, Mold and Connahs Quay Rail Tour of 29 April 1967. Behind are government-owned buildings that formed part of the Royal Ordnance Valley Works. Photograph Norman Parker.

In bright sunshine, the pair of specially cleaned Stanier 2-6-4Ts, 42616 and 42647, are approaching Bellan, between Mold and Rhydywym. This was the last passenger working to reach Rhydymwyn.

The tour breasts the top of Kinnerton bank near Hope & Penyffordd. This railtour originated at Crewe and arrived on the Mold branch via a circuitous route via Middlewich and Mouldsworth to Hooton where the two Stanier tank engines took over for the run, via Chester, to Rhydymwyn. The train is running 'wrong line', the normal 'down' line being secured out of use awaiting lifting. Had the leaning heads known it, after 118 years, this was the last time a passenger train would climb the 1 in 43 Kinnerton Bank. The tour returned from Rhydymwyn to Crewe via Hope Junction, Wrexham, Llangollen, Bidston, Chester (Liverpool Road) and then regained its original, outward path to Crewe. The tour, which involved four steam locomotives, was rated very highly by its participants despite a coach sustaining three hot axleboxes at Bidston!

Standard Class 4 4-6-0 75033 of Mold Junction departs from Mold with the 5pm Denbigh to Chester (General) on 28 April 1962, the last day of passenger services. The building in the background, a grain store, had once been an engine shed. Photograph Michael Mensing.

More of the tour. The 2-6-4Ts and their seven coach excursion is passing Bellan, between Mold and Rhydwymwyn. This was the last ever passenger train to reach Rhydymwyn. Photograph John Goss.

Mold Junction shed, viewed from the road bridge in September 1963, demonstrating how the close the building and yard lay to the by now disused platforms of Saltney Ferry station. By this time the shed was used by LMR and WR locos, as the presence of 7907 MARL HALL shows, standing amongst Black Fives, Fairburn tanks and so on. Photograph Brian Cowlishaw.

Chapter Thirteen
Royal Rites and Mold Branch Finale

Freight traffic over the Mold Junction to Hope Junction section of the original Mold Railway continued until 2nd February 1970 when the line was taken out of use, remaining traffic gaining access to Mold via the south to west curve at Penyffordd, from the Wrexham-Bidston line. The 1970 closure of the Mold Junction to Hope Junction section was of little consequence to Hawker Siddeley Aviation who had taken over the former de Havilland aircraft works at Broughton. The reception sidings, installed for the original users, Vickers, in 1939, were already out of use by July 1969, pending removal, although the 40hp John Fowler 0-4-0 diesel locomotive supplied new still existed, out of use, within the hangars. In April 1975 the locomotive was acquired by the then Flint & Deeside Railway Preservation Society and before moving to Llangollen station, was stored briefly at Oswestry. Named 'Eliseg' at Llangollen, the locomotive pioneered the first track relaying at the station but was then retired at Pentrefelin Sidings, between Llangollen and Berwyn on the expanding Llangollen Railway. In 2009 'Eliseg' had moved to Llanerchymedd,

as part of a project to re-open the Gaerwen to Amlwch line on Angelsey.

Traffic between Mold Junction yard and Rhydymwyn had remained steam worked, under trip notice, with Mold Junction's Stanier 'Black 5s' and 8Fs predominating Sulzer Type 2 (later Class 24 and 25) 1,160hp Bo-Bo diesels heralded the elimination of regular steam working as from late 1967. However Mold Junction marshalling yard continued to function and remained as a booking-on point for train crews for some years.

As the last of Mold Junction's steam locomotives drifted away to work out their final months of operation elsewhere, the traffic and facilities they had served also disappeared under a relentless programme of railway rationalisation. Local goods depots and sidings were being abandoned at an alarming rate. BR withdrew freight facilities at Mold on203rd April 1972, the once busy goods yard that held up to 231 wagons falling into disuse. While the empty sidings slumbered into decay, the streets through Mold shook under the weight of heavy lorries en route to nearby quarries. The same picture

applied at Rhydymwyn with rusty rails and weed-choked track leading to still busy Hendre quarries just beyond the station. The introduction of new, higher capacity, four-axle lorries to take Hendre limestone products away by road had meant the end of the 'Prestwin' wagon-load traffic in 1967. As a consequence the section from the Synthite works to Dolfechlas Crossing was closed as from 1st January 1968 but as late as 1973 rusting signal arms still hung from their posts long after any regular traffic had ceased. By and large, local people could be forgiven that a railway through Mold, hanging by a thread, still existed.

But trains did return to Rhydymwyn in the summer of 1974 with the arrival of Class 25 Bo-Bo 1,250 hp diesel locomotives, conveying large steel pipes for the Angelsey-Ellesmere Port oil pipeline which ingeniously uses part of the abandoned trackbed near Caerwys. Before burying beneath the old track formation, the pipes were stored in the former goods yard at Rhydymwyn until required. Thereafter the line from the Synthite works to Rhydymwyn slipped back into decay until 1978 when track-lifting commenced

Mold Junction on Sunday 1 May 1960 with Newport's Grange 4-6-0 6838 GOODMOOR GRANGE standing on No.1 road. Stabled on No.3 road is 3F 0-6-0T 47673, a type known locally as a 'Humpy'; it is so placed to be first engine off the shed in the early hours of Monday morning to perform the 'West End yard shunt', marshalling wagons for the first three freight departures of the day from Mold Junction yard. Behind 47673 stands Shrewsbury's BR Class 5 73037. Mold's own Black 5 4-6-0 45042 stands behind 6838 on No.2 road. The chimney protruding from the rear of the shed belongs to the sand drying plant. Photograph R.S. Carpenter.

Two Black Fives, led by 45316, take a Holyhead train past Saltney Ferry station in September 1963. The two tracks either side of the camera position were the up and down lines to Mold. We are looking towards Chester. Photograph Jim Peden.

Mold Junction line-up on 1 August 1960. From left, WR 2-8-0 2889, Hall 6958 OXBURGH HALL, Black 5 45412, 2-6-4T 42599, Hall 4937 LANELAY HALL, WD 2-8-0 90147, Black 5 45275, WR 2-8-0 3802 and Black 5 45031. 3802 appears to have travelled furthest; St Blazey in Cornwall was its home shed at that time. Photograph Jim Peden.

Saltney Ferry station in June 1959, looking west from the Saltney Lane bridge. Covered steps lead down to the island platform and wooden hut, serving as a booking office and waiting room. The down line of the Mold branch is immediately below the camera. To the left is Mold Junction engine shed with its coaling plant, the only one in North Wales. To the right of the coaling tower is the marshalling yard while in the distance the hangers of Hawarden aerodrome are visible. On the right of the picture a Class 3 0-6-0T can be seen shunting in the slate wharf sidings. In the early 1950s there were four shunting links here, Slate Yard, East Yard, West Yard and Mold Yard. In 1948 seven 0-6-0Ts were employed at Mold Junction but by 1965 the number had dropped to two, supplanted by three 0-6-0 diesel mechanical shunters. Up to and beyond the turn of the century Mold Junction was an increasingly important railway centre, with its own railway community; the terrace houses on the right are Ewart Street and North Street. Photograph Mowat Collection.

6964 THORNBRIDGE HALL stands between 8F 2-8-0 48246 and WD 2-8-0 90147 at Mold Junction on 1 August 1960. Photograph Jim Peden.

to a point just beyond the Synthite works at Mold. The honour of the la st ever train to leave Rhydymwyn station fell to Class 25 Bo-Bo diesel No. 25160 which hauled away a train load of redundant sleepers on 13th December 1978. On its way back to Mold 25160 passed a 1919 built 4wDM Simplex diesel (works No.1944) which continued to shunt tank wagons containing methanol at Synthite Ltd. Methanol was used in the production of formaldehyde. All traffic to Synthite Ltd was worked under local trip notice, using Sulzer Class 24 or 25 Bo-Bo diesel locomotives with occasional appearances of the larger English Electric 1Co-Co1 2,000hp Class 40 diesels. Sometimes demand at Synthite warranted no more than a solitary tank wagon, which, coupled to a lengthy Class 40, must have presented an odd spectacle.

At 4.37pm on Friday, 21st May 1976 the signalman on duty at Penyffordd signalbox, on the former Great Central Wrexham-Bidston line, looked out upon the deep claret livery of the royal train, the nine coaches, conveying the Queen and her entourage, being pulled at walking pace onto the spur leading to the Mold branch by an immaculate Class 40 diesel locomotive.

The opening earlier in the day of the prestige Theatr Clwyd arts complex at Mold by the Queen had brought the royal train overnight from Euston to the Principality, with the stations at Wrexham General and the more modest Caergrwle, on the Wrexham-Bidston=2 0line, being used in the course of the day's engagements by the royal party; the former station at Mold was deemed unsuitable for a royal arrival by train. But the single line Mold branch, even in its last few years of existence, still had an important part to play in the royal intinerary, fulfilling the role, albeit for two hours, as a discreet stabling point for the locomotive, heater van and the nine coaches comprising of a power brake vehicle, restaurant car, saloon, sleeping car, saloon, dining saloon, two further saloons, and first class brake; this consist represented the full-length royal train.

As the red tail lamps of the first class brake coach disappeared around the spur towards Mold, the points to the rear of the train were clipped, detonators were placed on the track and a red danger signal was displayed in both directions. No other train movements would be allowed for the duration of the Queen's stay on the Mold

branch. Meanwhile the Penyffordd signalman received back the 'one train working staff' from the Officer-In-Charge of the royal train. This subsequently enabled two further class 40 diesels from Chester, which arrived at Penyffordd at 5.50pm, to proceed with great caution onto the Mold branch and couple up to the Penyffordd end of the royal train. An hour later the two diesels, their immaculate blue paintwork reflecting the efforts of the maintenance staff at Springs Branch, Wigan - the diesels ' home base - took the train back to Caergrwle where the Queen detrained for an evening reception at Hawarden Castle. Later, after turning the empty stock at Croes Newydd, Wrexham, the royal train passed Penyffordd again en route for Hawarden where the royal party boarded for the overnight journey back to Windsor, via Wrexham, Birmingham and Slough.

The contribution to the smooth running of the royal tour made by railway staff led to personal letters of thanks to all railwaymen concerned, and Driver J. Douggie of Chester, who had driven the train from Chester to Wrexham in the early hours of Friday was sent a cheque, from BR management at Crewe, for the princely sum of £2.

The survival of goods rail traffic through Mold prompted local councillors in 1982 to press for a reinstatment of rail passenger services from Mold to Penyffordd and thence to Liverpool, the idea being to bring Merseyside day trippers by rail to visit Mold and the surrounding countryside. Returning trains would take local residents on shopping expeditions to Liverpool. Sadly, the councillors' imaginative plans came to nothing and the line's fate was sealed when the Synthite works terminated delivery of chemicals by rail in March 1983.

The line was 'mothballed' for a long period, in the hope that it could be revived for further use, but in June 1985 it bowed to the inevitable. Using bulldozers, cranes and portable cutting equipment, demolition contractors from South Wales ripped up the heavily-rusted track. Rotten sleepers were burnt while much of the redundant bullhead rail was cut up for export to Italy as scrap. Even the Brymbo-built cast iron bridges over the Alyn river, west of Llong station, were not spared. Signal posts were felled, including the last ex-LNWR wooden post fixed distant signal, once visible from the A483, between

Llong and Mold. The modern, train crew-operated level crossing equipment near Llong and at Mold was dismantled for further use elsewhere. Casual onlookers and retired railwaymen whose lives were built around the railway could only look on with sadness. By December of that year the contractor's task was almost complete. The platforms at Llong were now railless. Mold station lingered on as a building materials centre until 1988 when the station and goods sheds were razed to the ground to make way for a large Tesco superstore.

As stated at the beginning, rail traffic to Synthite Ltd ceased in March 1983 and the entire Chester-Denbigh line has now passed into history although the railway has not been forgotten by local people. Standing on the up platform at the erstwhile Hope & Penyffordd station (now owned by a railwayman) is an immaculate lower-quadrant signal. If passing motorists on the adjacent A55020express surprise or curiosity, then supporters of the LNWR will wince for the signal came from Wrexham and is pure GWR!

In 2002, and located further west, at Sodom, near Bodfari, the Denbigh and

Mold Junction Railway Society briefly established an 11 acre preservation site, including a third of a mile of the old trackbed towards Mold, terminating at the rear of the Aberwheeler Nursery garden centre, where a halt would be built. The long term aim was to eventually re-open a three mile stretch of track from Bodari to Afonwen. History was made at Sodom on Sunday, 13th January 2002, when the first standard gauge passenger vehicle to appear on the line in nearly 40 years arrived. With the help of Army regulars and volunteers from the 119th REME, based at Prestatyn, M56160, a 1957 Park Royal unpowered diesel multiple unit trailer car, was safely winched down on to its length of track. Present among the crowd of onlookers was Mr Pennant, great grandson of Capt Pennant who had done so much at Bodfari to get the Mold and Denbigh Junction Railway promoted and built in the 1860s.

The former British Rail vehicle had strong links with North Wales, as the Park Royal type saw widespread use over the Chester and Holyhead and Cambrian main lines until the mid-1970s. If the Chester to Denbigh line had stayed open then diesel multiple units

Mold Junction shed on a sunlit 7 February 1966, with only a few weeks to go before closure on 18 April. Visible To the left is the main Chester and Holyhead main line, the lattice post home and distant signal controlling trains on the down Mold line. The disused and decaying Saltney Ferry station is at the left with Saltney Lane bridge behind. The actual location and name Mold Junction has in the past brought confusion; some believed the shed was at Mold, ten miles away, while even an official LMS map, giving the geographical locations of the company's motive power depots, shows it just south of Mold where Mold and Tryddyn Junction should be! Photograph Sidney Wainwright.

like M56160, based at Chester, would have been employed on Denbigh services.

Sadly, by 2003, the Bodfari preservation project had to be wound down for various reasons; the Chester Chronicle's 1962 'old Aunty Emily' will have to await another time for a fresh come-back along the beautiful Wheeler Valley.

In conclusion, had the 1914 Bodfari Curve been built, the Chester-Denbigh line would have gained more importance as a diversionary route by taking some of the heavy summer Saturday Rhyl excursion traffic away from the often congested two track section between Connah's Quay and Flint on the Chester to Holyhead main line. As it remained, the Denbigh line was very much a local affair, but nevertheless a popular and useful link, in its heyday, between rural North Wales and industrial Northern England.

Above. **Long serving Mold Junction Engines 1: Sparkling in a fresh coat of black paint Mold Junction's 4F 0-6-0 M4065 is running in after a general overhaul in 1948 shortly after nationalisation. 4Fs were repaired either at Horwich or Derby. The numberplate sports the short-lived prefix 'M' for the newly-formed London Midland Region of British Railways. Later the clumsy 'M' was dropped and an additional '4' added but old company habits died hard and all through BR days shed staff and crews would refer to ex-LMS engines by their former company numbers. Thus M4065 and later 44065 would always be known as '4065'. Built in 1925 by North British, this locomotive served at Mold Junction through the 1950s but was withdrawn at Workington, in January 1965.**

Right. **A distinguished visitor; in August 1965 the sole surviving Royal Scot 46115 SCOTS GUARDSMAN comes slowly on to Mold Junction shed, past the Mold Jct No2 signal box which controlled access to the shed yard. The locomotive had brought in a freight from Carlisle Kingmoor. Relegated to goods work, 46115 was reportedly in poor condition but still commanded great affection from staff and enthusiasts alike. Mr Jack Robinson, shedmaster at Mold Junction, came out to welcome 46115 to 'Spike', the shed's long-standing nickname. In their heyday, the Royal Scots were very much part of the North Wales railway scene, although none was allocated to Mold Junction. Photograph E.N. Kneale.**

Mold Junction shed. Driver Bill Roberts (left) stands with (left to right) Lez Macey, Jack Fiddler and Colin Parry (Apprentice) in front of Jubilee 4-6-0 45572 EIRE of Bristol Barrow Road shed. Photograph Cleveland Jones.

It was unusual to see pannier tanks shunting at Mold Junction but Croes Newydd's 9610 is one, drawing a raft of wagons onto the East End headshunt opposite the closed platform of Saltney Ferry station. Photograph E.N. Kneale.

Grange 4-6-0 6836 ESTEVARNEY GRANGE rests between Mold Junction No.2 box and the coaling plant at the shed in March 1963. Sister locomotive 6821 LEATON GRANGE stands behind. She was a long-serving Plymouth (Laira) engine but ended her days at Worcester, being withdrawn in March 1965. Photograph E.N. Kneale.

A driver's view from the cab of a Mold Junction 'Humpy' on the east side of Saltney Lane overbridge next to Mold Junction shed. A North Eastern Region, Mirfield-based Austerity, 90593, is about to come alongside with an up mineral train. Photograph Cleveland Jones.

Mold Junction shed on 1 August 1960. GW 2-8-0 2889 of Hereford stands alongside Hall 6958 OXBURGH HALL of Pontypool Road. Photograph Jim Peden.

The railwayman's best friend: Davy Jones enjoys a brew on the footplate of a Standard 3F 0-6-0T, a 'Humpy'. The engine is on the Slate Yard shunt. Photograph Cleve Jones.

Photographed from a passing Holyhead to Manchester express, a grimy Birkenhead Crab 2-6-0 gets the once-over from its fireman as the engine stands on the up Mold to Chester line at Mold Junction, just beyond the now-closed Saltney Ferry station platform. Photograph E.N. Kneale.

Long Serving Mold Junction Engines 2: Homeward bound for Mold Junction, Black 5 45275 leaves Crewe with a freight on 2 September 1950. 45275, along with later-built 44800, was highly regarded by footplate staff at '6B'. Built by Armstrong Whitworth in 1936 as LMS 5275 this engine spent almost its entire BR career at Mold Junction, only being transferred away after closure of the shed in April 1966. Here she is in early BR unlined black livery; she was withdrawn for scrap at Rose Grove shed, near Burnley, in October 1967.

A 'Sunday afternoon' view of Mold Junction shed in May 1938, showing the depot's predominately freight locomotive allocation. Taken from the top of the coal stack, the photographer has caught ex-L&NWR G2 0-8-0s, LMS 4F 0-6-0s at rest, while on Nos. 2 and 3 roads a Stanier Black 5 4-6-0 rubs shoulders with an ex-works LMS 3F 0-6-0T.

Mold Junction, looking towards Rhyl, with a Britannia on the 4.10pm Holyhead-Birmingham train in September 1963. Photograph Brian Cowlishaw.

A 'Humpy' at Mold Junction. Standard 3F 0-6-0T 47410 shunts the slate yard at Mold Junction. Beyond lies Ewart Street, built by the LNWR for railway employees. Photograph Brian Cowlishaw.

Patriot Class 4-6-0 45520 LLANDUDNO passes through Mold Junction marshalling yard, c1960/1. The engine is facing west. In the distance is the John Summer's steel works at Shotton. Photograph Brian Cowlishaw.

4F 0-6-0 44589 ambles along the down Mold line, approaching the road bridge above Mold Junction shed. Photograph Brian Cowlishaw.

At 1 o'clock in the morning, 6982 MEMBERBY HALL of Bristol Bath Road is standing inside Mold Junction shed, about 1961. Photograph E.N. Kneale.

Chapter Fourteen
Mold Junction Memories

A portrayal of the Chester to Denbigh branch line would not be complete without an insight into the contribution made by Mold Junction engine shed. Although situated and contained within the down side curve at the beginning of the original Mold branch, the eight road depot was of main line status, reflected in its radius of operation which went far beyond North Wales. Engines, wearing the '6B' shedcode on the smokebox door, ranged far and wide and away from the North Wales coast. They were to be found in action to the north over Pennine moorland, through industrial Liverpool and Manchester, Lancashire, Derbyshire and Cheshire and finally south among the rolling countryside of the Welsh Marches. Some 6B engines, through operational reasons, even reached holiday destinations on the sunny south coast of England. During a critical shortage of express engines on the Western Section of the Southern Region in 1953, one of Mold Junction's Stanier Black 5s, No.45130, was even loaned to Nine Elms shed and had a taste of 'top link' running out of London's Waterloo station to Salisbury, Southampton and Bournemouth.

Behind the machines came the men who drove, fired and serviced them. In his own words, Owen J. Hughes gives his personal account of life at Mold Junction: 'I transferred from Chester West to Mold Junction in 1952 as a Registered Fireman who were allowed one more move in their grade to their chosen depot. I previously had spells at Shrewsbury, Crewe, Llandudno Junction (where I started as a cleaner) and finally came back to Chester in 1966 due to the partial closure of Mold Junction shed. I chose to move to Mold Junction because it was nearer to my home (a cycle ride away). I had mixed feelings initially about the transfer – a matter of adapting to freight trains, involving irregular and uncertain hours after years of firing on passenger and express freight with reasonable booking on/off times although I had had my share of goods work as well.

'It gave me a tremendous amount of job satisfaction though it was very hard work, leaving one physically exhausted after many a trip. As for life at Mold Junction in general, where do I start? No better way than midnight, December 31st. It had been the practice at Mold Junction for staff on duty on New Year's Eve to take up their positions on each loco in steam and at the stroke of midnight the place would erupt to the sound of engine whistles, from the deep but loud hooting of the Class 8s to the shrill whistles of the smaller engines, blending to make a noise that was joyously terrific and yet each with its own particular message of goodwill for the New Year. On occasions a passing

The wreckage of a Royal Navy Sea Venom jet fighter lies on the runway at Broughton after striking a stationary steam locomotive while coming into land over Mold Junction marshalling yard in 1954. Airfield policemen look on as the highly inflammable jet fuel is pumped out of the port wing in the foreground. Both engine and aircraft crew escaped serious injuries.
Photograph BAE Systems

train would hoot its own reply and join in the celebrations. Drivers asleep at home, partially awakened by the sound simply turned over, snug in the knowledge of a few more hours sleep before duty called. Other engine sheds had been prevented from greeting the New Year in this way due to noise complaints. As far as I am aware no such protests were made by anyone living near 6B. This is understandable perhaps because most of the local residents had at least one member of the family employed by the railways, living in railway-owned houses.'

Mold Junction Motive Power Depot, 6B

'An eight road shed. One odd feature in its layout was that No.8 road was nearest the main line, totally opposite to the recognised practice at other sheds of having No.1 road nearest the main line. On occasions a 'foreign' set of men diagrammed to 'pick up' an engine at 6B would first report to the Running Shift Foreman (RSF) and having ascertained off the engine board nearby that their engine was stabled on No.1 road would instinctively walk towards No.8 to the obvious delight of any onlookers.'

Vacuum-worked turntable

'Sometimes the turntable (now preserved) was out of commission for three or four days. The facts were widely publicised to all locomotive sheds concerned in order to give due notice to 'foreign' drivers needing to turn their engines at Mold Junction for their return diagrammed work. In such circumstances the triangle of lines at Mold Junction was used for turning. The move could involve all four signal boxes via the busy West End Yard situated between No.4 and No.3 boxes. Not surprisingly, permission at busy times could not always be granted. Alternatively engines were sent to Chester to turn via the triangle at No.5 box.'

Single Ashpit Road

'The fire-dropper fed clinker, ash and so on through a grid on the ashpit floor into a tub below (on rails). When full, it would be hauled upwards by means of a steel rope to the top and turned over to empty its contents into a wagon although sufficient water would have been poured into the tub initially to quench the hot contents. A sprinkler system immediately above the wagon was also available if needed. The wagon was then suitably labelled by the clerk in charge before departure. On occasions, due to the jostling received during transit to the East Yard, the wagon, if its contents showed any hint of steam or smoke, was rejected as unfit for traffic by the yard staff and returned to the shed, much to the annoyance of the fire dropper.'

Concrete Coaling Plant, Single Hopper

'The filling of the hopper was the duty of the firedropper on day work. A single wagon of coal, coupled up and drawn forward by means of a steel rope, was attached to a revolving capstan wheel. The loaded wagon was placed on an isolated 'table' and firmly secured to it with brakes pinned down. It was lifted bodily upwards to the top of the coaling plant and inverted to unload its contents into the hopper. The capstan wheel was operated by means of a foot plunger near by. Much fun was derived at times (especially from the younger element or even the young at heart in jocular mood) waiting for the opportunity for someone to sit on the capstan wheel. Unbeknown to the victim, the switch was restored to 'on' and the result can be left to the imagination. During construction of the coaling plant, a workman fell off but landed in a heap of sand. Cleaners with nothing else to do would climb up the coaling plant via the fixed ladders or stairway. They would then travel downwards by hitching a ride on the freshly-emptied coal wagons, much to the alarm of the men on the ground. When the new Running Shift Foreman's office and booking on point was built outside the shed in 1965 any tomfoolery by the juniors would be dealt with more emphatically with the offenders probably sent home'.

Shed Turners' Link

'A link of four weeks, worked in rotation; a six day, 48 hour week, with booking on times at 6.0am, 2.0pm and 10.0pm. There was also a Sunday duty, booking on at 8.0am. An additional week's work was taken up with the shed shunt duties, booking on time 8.0am. Shunting engines (typically a 3F 0-6-0T) would generally be allocated to this work. Its duties were to shunt out and collect empty coal wagons and loaded clinker wagons and trip them to East End Yard. The return trip brought in loaded coal wagons together with any miscellaneous traffic for the shed such as a stores van and/or wagons of sand or brake blocks. A shunter was in attendance when tripping wagons was in progress. The return journey was allowed to travel 'wrong road' to the shed.'

Coal quality and supply

'Mold Junction always had a good supply of coal in hand, its quality ever under strict scrutiny by 6B enginemen. There was ample space for stabling coal wagons. Mold Junction received a varied selection of coal from different pits, Gresford, Ifton, Point of Ayr, Hollybank (best coal) and Silverdale with the best type, overall, being 'Hard Yorkshire'. This type of coal was supplied mainly to passenger sheds and especially suited LMS engines. Ifton coal was less popular as it contained 'brass' veins which caused clinker. GW engines

thrived on soft 'Blind Coal'. On the occasions when 6B had deliveries of the same the shunt driver would single out each wagon and place in between two wagons containing inferior quality coal and thus it was fed into the hopper. When arranging vehicles in this way, he would also work on the principle of 'first loaded wagon to arrive, first to be emptied'. In doing so it would eliminate the risk of paying 'demurrage', a penalty imposed on wagons held for long periods of time.

'It was not unknown for Holyhead shed to run short of coal. In consequence, and by arrangement with Control, a supply of 'Best Yorkshire' would be grudgingly despatched on the first available goods. From time to time excess tonnage of coal available meant it would be stacked and later, during a period of imminent shortage, reloaded into wagons and used. The stacking of coal was done by a small number of shed staff on a voluntary basis together with casual labour – one man per wagon and shovels provided. This work was carried out on a Sunday, a quiet day at 6B.

'One such volunteer would be ex-main line driver Sam Jones, 60ish and 'brought off' footplate duties by the Medical Officer due to defective colour vision. In such cases (by long-standing agreement) enginemen would retain a driver's rate of pay and would also be found suitable work on the shed, in this instance as shed labourer. It was a job Sam readily accepted. Duties were sweeping the shed floor, keeping the pits clean with plenty of opportunities to work overtime. This appealed to his industrious and enterprising nature. So by working 10 to 12 hours per day, perhaps for weeks on end, he became the first employee to earn £1,000 in 12 months at 6B, quite an achievement in those days. I recall his memorable saying that he earned more handling a brush than he did handling the regulator. It certainly raised a few eyebrows – others simply turned colour!'

Saturday and weekend working

'All engines not required over the weekend until Monday were disposed of on the ashpit, fires cleaned out, ashpan raked clean and smokebox cleared of ash. The Running Shift Foreman, in conjunction with Engine Control, would allocate each engine (as they arrived on the shed) to cover diagrammed work on Monday. The relevant information was passed to the Shed Turner, who placed each engine off the ashpit on to shed roads, in their correct sequence for departure. First engine off the shed I recall was the 12.50am West End Yard shunter. It was important that this locomotive arrived in the yard on time to form-up the early morning freight trains bound for the North Wales coast, the first of which was the 2.6am Menai Bridge – any delay would set the phones ringing. Each shed road would be filled to its maximum length except for 4, 5 and 6 which were kept exclusively for engines due for washing out and engines marked down for repair.

'Locomotives for washing out on Sunday and Monday would need to occupy separate roads inside the shed, on the blocks. Engines with known repairs also had to be put first in. Needless to say these engines would be among the last to arrive on shed. Consequently the aforementioned roads could not be utilised for stabling purposes until such engines arrived on the scene. The result was to make life more difficult for the shed staff. Engines needing repair were always brought to a stand under the guidance of the fitter on duty, inside the shed. For convenience of work and for added protection, a gap of at least six feet was made between the locomotive due for repair and the next engine. Sometimes use was made of pinch bars and human muscle power to move locomotives out of steam. A pinch bar was a length of iron tapered at one end. By inserting it between rail head and wheel two or three men could move an engine a few inches to aid fitters or men conducting boiler washing. An example would be a wheel spoke preventing access to a washout plug.

'Mold Junction locomotives, under the direction of Mr Jack Robinson, Shed Master and able assistants Foreman Fitter Harold Edwards and Leading Fitter Fred Taylor, enjoyed a reputation among railwaymen for well-maintained engines, a fact not lost on 'foreign' sheds who often borrowed Mold Junction locomotives to cover their own diagrams. As a consequence, when the best Class 5s and 8Fs returned 'home' they were often overdue for washing out.

'On a late Saturday afternoon the main line driver, with his six hour docket safely tucked in his pocket, and eagerly anticipating an early finish for the first time that week, moves his engine towards the water column off the shed. Meanwhile, ahead on the ashpit, the hard-working Fire-Dropper eventually finishes his locomotive: "monster fire that, up to the brick arch, took 45 minutes to drop." On moving that engine forward the Shed Turner remarks: "there's another one behind like that one."

'Drivers were allowed ten minutes to make their engines secure after arrival on shed. Before leaving the footplate the driver would make certain the regulator was shut, handbrake was 'on' and cylinder cocks open, noting any defects to be attended to on the engine's record card. The Fire-Dropper in turn took charge of the engine for its disposal. The next engine would very soon be moved up from under the coaling plant for its disposal; thus each locomotive in the queue behind would be moved one up, turned on up or down line as required,

watered and coaled. 'Due to the sometimes lengthy process of moving engines forward on to the ashpit, and of injecting water into the boiler, the result could be a great loss of steam pressure. Putting fresh coal on the fire to increase steam pressure was prohibited for obvious reasons – the best reason of all being to avoid the wrath of the Fire Dropper. Thus, in its weakened state, the locomotive would be driven slowly to its designated place on the shed, the Shed Turner fully aware of its now reduced braking power. In some instances an engine, very low in steam and unable to move under its own power, would be coupled up from behind and pushed on to the shed road.

'So as not to cause undue delay to oncoming locomotives the process of moving engines towards the ashpit needed to be done as quickly as circumstances would permit, in order to allow an engine off the main line to squeeze in. Enginemen at 6B were very keen to finish their turn of duty on a Saturday, the last day of the unpopular afternoon work

'Filling water tanks proved time consuming, for very few engines arrived on shed with tanks full of water. Exceptions were L.E (light engines) from 'down the coast' to Mold Junction which filled up on Fflint troughs, for which the Shed Fireman was truly grateful.'

The Dreaded 'Block On'

'The turntable/ashpit area held only six or seven locomtives and congestion here could block access from main line to shed. The result was 'stalemate', waiting for engines requiring washouts to arrive. Nevertheless the Shed Turner, by moving the leading engines forwards and backwards, could still keep the firedropper active. In these circumstances the Running Shift Foreman/Shed Turner immediately informed the signalman at Mold Junction No.2 (which controlled movements on/off shed) of the prevailing situation, with an added request to divert the offending loco arriving for washout 'wrong road' or the wrong direction on to the shed and hence to the ashpit. The engine then by-passed the acknowledged route onto the shed and thus, happily for those concerned, would be installed first in the queue for washout.

'On receiving the instructions the signalman thereafter shunted each engine destined for the shed clear of the main line into a siding at nearby East End Yard – not a popular move with engine crews who were by this time in a position to observe every move made on the ashpit opposite, while anxiously awaiting a positive move up. Meanwhile the Shed Turner could always be relied upon to do his utmost to clear the backlog of engines as soon as possible. Once the engines for boiler washing were safely installed inside the shed the work of stabling other locomotives could begin in earnest. Finally, at the

end of an arduous turn of duty, driver and fireman made their separate ways home, leaving behind a shed full of 'dead engines' – quiet and still under the dimmed shed lights.'

Sunday work at Mold Junction and Enthusiast Visits

'The Running Shift Foreman would always oblige polite requests to walk round the shed to see the locomotives but with the usual warning to such visitors to take care.

'Booking on times on Sundays were as follows:
Running Shift Foreman: 8.0am-4.0pm
Shed Turner: 8.0am-4.0pm
Washer Out: 8.0am-4.0pm
Fitters(four): 8.0am-4.0pm
Steam Raiser: 2.0pm-10.0pm, 10.0pm 6.0am

'Until the advent of ex-GW men and engines in 1960 when Mold Junction became a 7-day shed with round the clock booking-on times, the only shed staff on duty after 4.0pm were the Steam Raiser and an Engine Fitter (although footplate staff occasionally worked main line on Sundays under 'red ink roster working'). Both men worked unsupervised but were no doubt properly briefed on matters in hand by the Running Shift Foreman and the two would have access to a telephone where they could exchange information with Engine Control should the need arise. Mold Junction had an allocation of 42 engines at the time and about 25 would be fired up on Sundays with the Steam Raiser solely responsible for raising steam, albeit at staggered times, for engine departures in the early hours of Monday. Steam Raisers were ex-footplate staff and ideally suited for this work, for they were practical men with a fair amount of knowledge of engine diagrams, which came in useful when talking to Engine Control.

'On Sunday mornings one would be aware of shunting movements on the shed due perhaps to unavoidable alterations to engine diagrams. After 2.0pm the Steam Raiser would be actively engaged in 'coaling the bars', a cute method of forming a nest-like heap of coal at the back of the firebox. Later, at 4.30pm lighted firelighters, two or three per engine on average, would be placed on the coal. Thus began the process of 'getting up steam'. Sometimes, when firelighters were in short supply, a paraffin patch was added to a firelighter. This was a cloth or rag soaked in used oil or paraffin. Miscellaneous items – firelighters, wheelbarrows, buckets and so on were stored in a building inside the shed at the end of No.8 road, adjacent to the men's cabin. The Engine Fitter was readily available to inject more water into the boiler, prior to firing up, if it was thought necessary.

'Unfortunately, raising steam in a large number of locomotives could not be carried out without the emission of great quantities of smoke. This often seemed to drift from the shed area towards the railway-owned terraced village of Saltney Ferry opposite. On such occasions the ever-alert occupants quickly gathered in their washing and closed windows against the menace. Sometimes, due to wind changes, the smoke would be carried or directed elsewhere, much to everyone's relief. No official protests were made against the smoke by the inhabitants of Saltney Ferry. To them perhaps, it had become an acceptable way of life.'

Wartime and the 'Yankees' Arrive

At one time, Mold Junction drivers, fireman and guards booked off work at several places, including Bangor, Rowsley (Derbyshire), Longsight (Manchester), Holyhead and even Warrington where there was a private lodge. During the Second World War, enginemen on duty were given extra rations; bully beef, biscuits and so on, handed out at the place where they stayed, away from home. Perhaps the food they had brought with them could be eaten at another time and place. Extra rations for serving railwaymen were codified thus: 'when war exigencies kept them on the track for long periods.' Long hours of duty had become a trade mark for railway footplate staff, especially those from freight depots like Mold Junction who were vital for the war effort.

Owen continues: 'I had a chat with an old colleague who worked as a fireman and later a driver at 6B during the last war when the 'Yankee' locomotives (S160 2-8-0s Nos.1918 and 1921) arrived. They came accompanied by two American fitters, who stayed for a while to instruct 6B men in their maintenance. Footplate staff swallowed as much information as possible about these seemingly complicated locomotives which indeed, they were, until you got used to them. Our own Class 5 Staniers looked very ordinary by comparison. For instance, a Driver was only allowed one hour to prepare a loco for train duty but on these American engines there was not an oiling cork to be seen. All oiling points had a screwnut – each had to be unscrewed with a spanner to oil. Sand boxes were placed high on the side of the boiler near the dome, making sand filling difficult for the fireman. For safety there was a handrail to hold on to. These engines had three separate brake systems. Westinghouse, vacuum and steam brake (ratchet type). Little wonder then that they were festooned with pipes – a Fitter's nightmare. They had no dip scoop, so water troughs were denied to them. The Yankee engines had two very reliable, and strong water injectors (live steam) and would very soon fill the boiler. I am told that a set of 6B men worked a freight train from Mold Junction Yard to Holyhead on one tender tank of water filled to the

maximum.'My old mate recalled that the ones at Mold Junction in 1943/44 had left-hand drive with a huge, vertical regulator, the handle of which was just above the reversing gear, in the driver's corner. When starting from scratch the driver had to be very careful. It was best that the reverser was placed in full forward or backward gear, 75%. Open the regulator (some used both hands, giving more feel) carefully, close and wait for movement. I know that this was the basic method of starting steam locomotives, but this particular class of engine needed extra care because the steam brake was slow acting. Should the engine shunt forward suddenly due to too much regulator, it would take some time to stop.'

'The slow acting steam brake was to lead, perhaps inevitably, to a serious accident at Mold Junction which can be related later. Owen relates his own encounter with a 'Yankee' 2-8-0: 'My single experience with this type of engine around this time (1943-44) was as a Passed Cleaner when at Llandudno Junction. We boarded a 'Yankee' at Chester. We were given instructions by the Crewe North men from whom we had taken over. The very first words the driver told us were; 'careful with the regulator and don't trust the brake', which summed it up really. Otherwise it was a treat to work on them. During the journey down the coast I watched my mate – he was as excited as a child with a new toy and never shy to sound the whistle/horn to draw attention. If only I had a camera in those days…'

Accidents

The railway was always a dangerous place and it was inevitable that accidents would occur to railwaymen while carrying out their tasks amid heavy machinery. One accident happened during wartime and concerned a 'Yankee' 2-8-0 and a firedropper's mate at Mold Junction. Owen takes up the story: 'It involved a young Irish lad, Jack Larkin. He was working underneath an engine on the ashpit. It was common practice for the firedroppers to turn on the water in the hosepipe and place it near the wheel before going underneath, into the pit, to rake out the ashpan. As he reached out for the hosepipe the engine he was working under was given an almighty push from behind. Unfortunately the wheel of the locomotive ran over his arm. The pain must have been tremendous but his shouting raised the alarm. In great distress, with blood everywhere, but showing outstanding courage and coolness, he picked up his severed arm and was escorted to the Running Shift Foreman's office where first aid was given, while awaiting an ambulance.

'It soon became known that the offending locomotive was a 'Yankee' that had been given too much throttle in the shed yard. Within the confines of stabled engines the slow acting steam

brake had not had the distance to stop in time.'

'Jack's horrible experience did not prevent him returning to railway work and he came back to Mold Junction shed to take up duties as a stores man. After closure of the shed in 1966 he continued the same duties at Chester Diesel Depot until his retirement.

Other men were not so lucky. '6B' had its share of tragedies and Owen Hughes recalls Driver Arthur Jones: 'While doing his mate a favour by climbing the tender steps to fill the tank, he overbalanced, fell and knocked his head on the buffers – Driver Jones must have died instantly. Foreman Williams was very quickly on the scene and almost as quick he returned to the Office to inform the powers that be. For those of us waiting to depart the shed, me included (I recall taking a light engine to Birkenhead) a lengthy stand seemed in prospect awaiting a doctor and the police.

'Suicides on the railway were an occupational hazard for engine crews but staff at Mold Junction were doubly shocked one day in 1954 when a Mold Junction Driver, who lived in Ewart Street, was found dead on the lines opposite the shed, having taken his own life; a farewell note gave family reasons for his decision.

Another incident, highly unusual and possibly unique, involved a Mold Junction locomotive and a low flying jet fighter in 1954. The West End of Mold Junction Yard lay very close to the main runway of Hawarden aerodrome. Aircraft would constantly take off and land over the yard and main line. Special emergency stop colour light signals, on the Chester and Holyhead main line, were located to the west and east approaches to Mold Junction. Normally unlit, the signals would give a red aspect in the unlikely event of an aircraft crashing onto the railway. But the signals could do little to stop an aircraft flying too low as it made its approach. Engine crews watched out for the rapidly approaching landing lights or listened for the distinctive scream of jet engines as aircraft conducted test-flights after construction at de Havilland's Broughton factory.

The plant built the distinctive twin boom design Vampire and Venom jet fighters in large numbers and they became well-known to shed and footplate staff at Mold Junction. Railwaymen also learnt, by way of rubbing shoulders with aircraft workers over a quiet pint or two after work, that certain test pilots might, for their amusement, try their luck at flying as low as possible and putting the frighteners on an unsuspecting engine crew just feet below the plane as it landed or took off.

On 16th July 1954 the inevitable happened: an engine with a stone train from Penmaenmawr was approaching

Mold Junction on the up slow line. The Driver, William Williams and his Fireman, William Roberts, both from Llandudno Junction, saw a de Havilland Sea Venom making its approach to land and by judging the height of the aircraft by the bright gleam from its landing lights they knew instantly that this oncoming jet was a bit too low for comfort. In fear for their lives, both driver and fireman threw themselves flat on the footplate as the Sea Venom screamed overhead, its wheels striking the top of the tender leaving, in Owen's words, 'the tread imprint of Dunlop on the tank vents'.

The brand-new aeroplane, which was completing a test flight for the Royal Navy, went on to make a belly landing on the airfield, sustaining extensive damage but fortunately without loss of life to its two-man crew. They were rushed to hospital at Chester suffering from spinal injuries. Witnessed by the signalman on duty at nearby Mold Junction No.4 signal box, news of the incident quickly spread by the internal railway telephone. By a narrow margin, both engine driver, fireman, test pilot and flight observer had escaped death.

Engine preparation for the 5.15am Mold Junction goods to Denbigh

Owen describes the preparation and working of an early morning freight diagram: 'We booked on at 4.0am and were allowed 45 minutes preparation time for our diagrammed locomotive, an LMS Standard 4F 0-6-0. On arrival at the shed we knew what to expect – thick black smoke from freshly lit-up engines blanketing the whole shed area, making walking up and down from the engine to stores to fetch oil and equipment difficult. On the engine footplate you would find a layer of soot that needed the attention of the engine hosepipe; a subsequent wipe down with cloths made life easier. We had a few early turns in our link, namely 1.0am to Patricroft, 2.16 to Menai Bridge and 2.57 to Crewe.

'With regard to the 5.15am it was important to arrive at work in good time for, apart from normal preparatory duties, we may had to move our engine over a pit for repairs, if one was available, which was all time consuming. The 4F had inside motion which could be reached for oiling (big end eccentric cranks and so on) by the Fireman only

by crawling on his belly between the frames and the underside of the boiler, with his legs sticking out. Again, if only we'd had a camera at the time…) The Fireman, incidentally, did the oiling for the Driver. I brought newspapers from home to lie on and any spare paper would be placed under our coats in the lockers on the tender footplate.

'It was important to inspect sandboxes and fill them if necessary. Sometimes fire irons were buried under the coal on the tender; they had to be dug out and reset on the tender so that they were easily accessible, if needed, en route. Finally, having topped up the tender tank and washed our hands with water on the shovel, we were ready for the road.

'Several locomotives were due off the shed around our departure time including our diagrammed bank engine, a Class 8 or Austerity 2-8-0, manned by Tom Caddy, our regular Kinnerton Bank Driver. Like the men from Wigan, Tom wore clogs at work with a thin layer of rubber on sole and heel. Quite a character Tom, you either did it or you didn't with him; a tall man who walked with shoulders back and with a

Saltney Ferry station in early BR days. In the foreground are the down fast and slow tracks of the Chester and Holyhead main line. In the background stands Mold Junction shed, coded 37 in LNWR days. From 1935 the code became 6B until closure in April 1966. The shed was rebuilt after the war, the decaying 'northlight' roof being reconstructed with a concrete louvre type roof. Resident 4F 0-6-0 44065 stands to the right while peering out is Chester Compound 41121. The tender of an Austerity 2-8-0 is also visible.

habit of placing both hands in his overall pockets at the front as he walked.

'I recall an incident which involved him when working a coal slack train from Hope Junction to Connah's Quay Power Station. The train had come to a stand at the top of 1 in 43 Kinnerton bank near the stop board. He was signalled by the Guard that he had sufficient brakes pinned down although the proper procedure was for the train to be moved forward slowly and the wagon brakes (always on loaded wagons) pinned down while still on the move. Tom shouted "I'll tell you when there's enough brakes pinned down – pin a few more down – I'm first through the crossing gates at Broughton!" No one would argue with that.

Tom would always give us a good push up the bank. He would come up with us as far as Penyffordd, where his engine would uncouple and return light to Mold Junction for further work.

'Leaving the shed at the correct time was always satisfactory, because we had been diagrammed to run before the 5.40am Chester to Denbigh passenger train and we dare not delay it or else there would be 'Please explain' papers flying around. We would proceed off the shed to Mold End Yard where we would attach the engine to the train and receive details from the Guard concerning train weight and number of wagons to be detached at Hope Junction and Mold. Pulling out of the yard we would then reach the starter signal and draw to a halt to await the bank engine. With a green light from the Guard in his brake van to tell us that the bank engine had coupled up, our goods train was ready to tackle Kinnerton bank.

'Soon and on time the starter signal and distant (for Broughton) showed green and my mate sounded two crow whistles from our engine, quickly repeated by the bank engine. The train moved steadily at first but by the time we reached Broughton, three quarters of a mile from the starter signals, one could say we were making a run for the bank ahead. My mate would not work the engine too hard initially, he would let the bank engine do most of the work until he reached the dip near Kinnerton. My Driver would then start pulling his share of the train for the 1 in 43 incline ahead. Kinnerton bank had three sets of trap points, the last of which was situated at Dodd's Sand Siding a short distance from the double arch road bridge near the summit.

'The sand siding was worked, I'm told, until the late 1940s and access was from the down side only. At this stage of the journey a steam locomotive was working under full pressure, a sound I shall always remember, particularly the tempo of escaping steam from the valves and pistons and the noise of the injectors singing and, I suppose, the sound of the Fireman's shovel hitting the firehole door ring. In the darkness of a winter morning, the glow from the firebox via the front ashpan lit up the whole area as we went along, illuminating frightened rabbits and even the odd fox going about its hunting on the embankments and cuttings of Kinnerton bank.

'Once we had reached the top of Kinnerton bank and providing that the distant signal for Penyffordd was in the 'off' position, the Guard would detach the bank engine while it was still on the move. As per Rules and Regulations the bank engine's shackle was always attached to the hook of the vehicle next to the engine which made it possible for the Guard to uncouple. He would simply lift the shackle off the hook by using his shunting pole (the shackle would be coupled up loose, not screwed up). The action of uncoupling was done by standing on the van steps – generally done by the younger element.

'Once this anti-Rules and Regulations act had been carried out, the Guard showed a white light to both Drivers (bank engine and train) which would normally be acknowledged by a 'pop' on the locomotive's whistle or hooter. This move was arranged beforehand between the engine crews – all fully conversant with the move. It was a matter of knowing your men – some would do it, others wouldn't. The purpose of this action was to save time. Otherwise the train would have to be brought to a halt at Penyffordd to uncouple the banker.

'Having done our work at Hope Junction and Mold, a good run to Denbigh was essential. We would be 'on the collar' to the summit at Star Crossing Halt. It would be a reduced train by that time but still plenty of tonnage for an ex-LMS Standard 4F 0-6-0. Very often we were glad to reach the top and then free-wheel to a little beyond Bodfari where the slight rise in gradient heralded the approach to Denbigh. The section between Caerwys and Bodfari on the down line was re-laid with concrete sleepers in the early 1950s. This gave me my first experience of running over concrete sleepered track. As can be imagined, the ride was very solid with no 'give' whatsoever.

'We arrived at Denbigh at approximately 6.43am booked time. Having run round our train and placed it in the up side yard we would then spend some time on the shed, turning the locomotive on the former Holyhead turntable, before filling the tank with water and examining the engine. It was always important to turn the engine first before taking water as a fully-laden tender would affect the balance of the turntable. By the time we had turned our locomotive the following 5.40am Chester to Denbigh passenger train would have arrived in the station.

'On our return to the goods yard, wagons forming the 8.35am to Mold Junction would be ready for us to back up to them. Then, with time to spare, we would climb into the brake van for breakfast and a chat with our Guard. A regular topic of conversation and laughter might be the 'Bodfari affair' mentioned earlier.'

Going Down to Broughton and Bretton
Kinnerton bank required skill, not only in going up with a bank engine at the rear but also coming down. An 8F or WD 2-8-0 with 40 or so loaded wagons of coal from the Wrexham area would leave the stop board at the top of Kinnerton bank with sufficient brakes pinned down on the front end of the train. The numbers would be determined by the Driver for the safe working down the 1 in 43 incline into Broughton and Bretton station.

On a train of this length and weight approximately ten wagon brakes would be pinned down by the Guard – usually every other wagon but he would make certain that the wheels could rotate. On rejoining his brake van in the rear he would then assist the Driver by applying the van hand brake while up in front on the tender brake could be applied separately.

During its descent the train had to be kept under strict observation – on both sides – by the engine crew. At times it was noticed that a pin that held the wagon brake handle in place had worked loose and out of its socket, leaving the brake handle jumping up and down like a demented kangaroo, as the saying goes. A loose brake handle had this universal effect if not secured in its proper place. In reality this meant that there was one less brake to hold the train and an engine crew didn't need any more like that. Another time smoke might be revealed from an overheated brake block, setting fire to an oily patch on the wagon underframe. This would soon fizzle out but added to this possible misery, of being engulfed in smoke, more often the Guard had to contend with coal dust billowing into his draughty van from the racing wagons in front. Goods Guards frequently complained about the amount of dust entering their vans.

The Driver had to keep a tight hold of his train, on its descent, to curb its speed until a point, which varied with the load, was reached beyond the double arched bridge on the Kinnerton side.

If all was well the train would be allowed to increase speed. This was achieved by gradually releasing the engine brake but leaving the tender brake on or perhaps easing it slightly and then only releasing fully to 'off' if the Driver thought that there was not enough momentum or speed for the train to overcome the rising gradient beyond Kinnerton. Once the train was over the top of this rise and in full view of Broughton Signal Box, with its crossing gates between (some three quarters of a mile away) the Driver applied the engine brake as required to bring his train to a stand near the stop signal protecting the crossing gates.

Here the Guard would climb down from his van and pick up the wagon brake handles before departure.

To motorists, sitting patiently in their stationary cars on the A55, which crossed the Mold line at Broughton and Bretton, the sight of smoke issuing from the overheated brakes of a wagon led them to believe that the train was on fire. The Signalman at Broughton, from his vantage point, reliably followed the approaching goods train's progress and he was ever alert to any distress signals from the crew. One engine driver remarked to the 'bobby' at Broughton, as a joke, that they would have a whip round to buy him a pair of binoculars. With a little smile and a wink the Signalman produced from a nearby drawer a large pair of binoculars!

The men from the 'Western' arrive at Mold Junction, April 1960
'Oh what a glorious sight to see,
Western men cycling down Hough Green,
26 sets on 52 bikes,
The Green Carders in the rear,
On motorised trikes.........'
Dickie Darlington, '6B' popular poet and prankster

The transfer of Western Region enginemen and their jobs from Chester West shed (which closed for conversion to a diesel depot) brought great changes to Mold Junction, the most important being the advent of seven-day working for men. The 'Green Carders' referred to in the poem were Drivers and Firemen placed on 'Considerate Duties', owing to personal circumstances or disabilities. Considerate Duties would include shed shunting and engine preparation. One Green Carder who didn't move to Mold Junction was a Driver with one eye. Owen J. Hughes had known Gron Ephraim at school and both joined the railways at the same time, Owen starting his footplate career at Llandudno Junction under the LMS and Gron similarly at Chester for the GWR. Later in life Gron suffered an eye infection and it was necessary for it to be removed in an operation in order to save the other one.

Owen completes the story: 'On his return to duty he was taken off the main line and placed as a Fireman in the shed link – don't ask me why he was retained as a footplate man, benevolence at the time perhaps. When I saw the list of men due to be transferred from Chester West to Mold Junction I was surprised to see Gron Ephraim's name included. The powers that be, however, decided against sending him to Mold under the 'considerate work' system and I personally was secretly gratified by their action because I knew that having to travel to 6B from his home in Chester would have caused Gron great stress. The next man senior to Gron volunteered for the move and Gron

remained at Chester West, where he was promoted to Driver as per seniority in due course'.

The ex-GW Chester men brought their own talk and dress habits and this caused some banter among die-hard ex-LMS footplatemen. Cleve Jones, an LM fireman who started as a cleaner at Mold Junction in 1954 remembered one incident: 'One day someone put a placard outside the stores which said "Western men collect your Swindon braces, feeders etc. here", together with a collection of Western paraphernalia on view. Western men rarely used bib and brace overalls like the LM did, but trousers and braces – in this area anyway. The talk was different too; "feed" instead of injector for instance; "feeder" meant oil can, "board" for signal arm or "peg" and so on. For myself I was glad they came, a chance to sample GW engines. Personally I liked them; they rode so steadily and everything on the footplate worked! A good solid job, like nearly everything GW. My first trip was on a 28XX 2-8-0; it could pull a house down.'

Cleve continues: 'There was much of a partisan spirit among the men, London Midland versus Western Region but the Western men settled in nicely. I can remember a conversation between a Western Driver (pointing to a 'Hall' 4-6-0 on shed) and his LM counterpart – "I don't care what you say, a 'Hall' in good nick is as a good as a 'Black 5'" – not realising he was paying a compliment! For fast freight, the 'Granges' were a superb job and GW engines generally rode well. I have been on a 'Castle' with speeds in the 90s at Baschurch on the Chester to Shrewsbury line but the engine rode like a coach. We had a 'Castle' or 'County' 4-6-0 on the 3.15 Paddington, working as far as Shrewsbury.'

Mold Junction shed now had more of everything, men, extra turns of duty, engines – and consequentially more smoke. The shed was now 'open all hours' and the increased level of smoke inevitably led to serious complaints from local residents. Protests were made to railway management, the Flintshire County Council and local MP Mrs Irene White who took up the matter with the British Transport Commission. At this time housing in Saltney Ferry had become council owned and many new non-railway faces were to be seen around. In order to be 'good neighbours', every effort was made by railwaymen to minimise the smoke emissions. More engines were kept in steam over the weekend in order to avoid having to re-light them. Notices to remind staff about smoke were posted around the shed and Running Shift Foremen were on their toes, looking out for careless or excessive emissions from locomotives. In spite of the precautionary measures, two irate housewives, pushing prams, burst into the shed one day and demanded to see

the Shedmaster. The enraged mothers made their points loud and clear to the effect that doors and windows facing the shed had always to be kept shut and that clothes on the washing line were being spoilt.

Smoke complaints in the Chester district, as a whole, were on the increase. Chester 'Top Shed', increasingly surrounded by new housing estates in the Tarvin area of the City was also bombarded with grievances. Steam sheds, so long a familiar part of urban life, were well and truly under the hammer. The removal of steam locomotives from Chester West was good news for the residents of the adjacent Hoole district but bad for those living in Saltney Ferry.

Dealing with smoke complaints from angry women was one item on the busy daily agenda for Mold Junction's 'Boss', Mr Jack Robinson. Mr Robinson had taken up the appointment of Shedmaster at Mold Junction in late 1951, taking over from long serving Shedmaster Mr Crofts. Jack Robinson was the grandson of the famous Ben Robinson, who made railway history in August 1895 with an epic run between Crewe and Carlisle, at the regulator of Precedent Class 2-4-0 'Hardwicke' during the Railway Races to the North. The railway ran deep in the Robinson family and Jack himself was to serve for forty years. He started his apprenticeship on the LNWR at Willesden in 1919 and was a lifelong pal of Max Dunn, another LNWR apprentice and enthusiast who eventually became Shedmaster at Bangor as well as becoming a well-known railway author and preservationist. Prior to his appointment as Shedmaster at Mold Junction, Mr Robinson had been Examining Fitter at Llandudno Junction.

Under Mr Robinson's direction, Mold Junction's own locomotives were always kept well-maintained but diagrammed Western Region engines, on arrival at Mold Junction shed, were found to be in a poor state, often with blocked tubes and tubeplates. The locomotives concerned mainly came from Oxley shed at Wolverhampton. It transpired that Oxley was sending its worst engines to Mold Junction. This meant needless extra labour for Mold Junction shed staff in getting them serviceable for their return diagrammed workings.

Matters came to a head and WR engines known to be in need of repairs were immediately sent back light to their home depots leaving Control to find replacement locomotives and crews to work traffic to the Western Region. Sparks began to fly but Mr Robinson's tactics paid off. After a while, improvements were noticed and suitable, better kept WR engines began to arrive at Mold Junction and at all points in between.

Sadly Mr Robinson, like his famous forebear, never had a well-earned retirement after a lifetime on the railways. The decline of the steam locomotive on British Railways was hard for him to bear and the final years of Mold Junction engine shed were exceedingly grim and unrewarding, with frustration often leading to despair. For example, one day in November 1965 the stores van arrived from Crewe with some desperately needed Class 5 brake blocks. On unloading them the fitters were somewhat perplexed to find that the brake blocks were not recognisable. Mr Robinson was consulted and he despairingly realised that they were old LNWR George V brake blocks! On another occasion he found an ex-Great Western '2800' 2-8-0 with a cracked frame. To his astonishment he saw that some individual had tried to 'repair' the frame by bolting a pair of rail fishplates either side of the fissure!

Perhaps it was all too much. In January 1966 Jack Robinson collapsed in his office. Driver Norman Barber, a first-aider, made him comfortable while awaiting an ambulance. He lived for another year, just long enough to return with his son Anthony to view the shed and meet friends and colleagues, just prior to closure. Driver Barber was no stranger to drama and tragedy; he and his fireman had watched in horror, when owing to a signalling error at Baschurch station in February 1961, a 'Hall' 4-6-0 smashed, at speed, into the rear of their stationary goods locomotive, killing the crew and a railway storeman travelling in the first coach of a Chester to Wolverhampton passenger train. The accident was the most serious involving a Mold Junction engine crew and guard.

The Mold Junction Breakdown Team and Fire Brigade

Mold Junction was allocated its own breakdown train and gang to deal with any incident. Owen J. Hughes takes up the story: 'Our shedmaster would on occasions be summoned to the shed or in railway jargon 'called out' when off duty for any emergency that needed his personal supervision such as derailments involving engines or wagons wherever they might be within the 6B area. Once the engine and breakdown van with all the crew aboard left the shed, the gang would settle down to enjoy a game of dominoes – probably the highlight of the trip.

'Pat Grunwood, a Fitter, was a regular member of the breakdown gang as well as being a member of the 6B Fire Brigade. Under the supervision of Mr Robinson the brigade practised regularly but their only claim to fame was that they never once dealt with a fire! But they were paid annually for their extra duty.'

'Pat recalled having to climb the ladder, under the watchful eye of the 'Boss', to the top of the coaling plant to deal with a large lump of coal that had lodged in the hopper aperture. Armed with a long shunting pole he began to prod the offending lump in order to release some two tons of coal. Working thus from the tiniest of platforms he was fortunate that height didn't bother him. Had he lost his balance the consequences would have been serious indeed.

'Eventually he succeeded, with the whole tonnage of hitherto trapped coal falling with a loud crash into the empty hopper while the resultant cloud of coal dust seemed to hover over the hopper's aperture for ages where Pat stood. He survived holding a white cloth to his face. His training as fireman in the Mold Junction Fire Brigade had paid dividends at last. Another story that I recall him telling me was that he always looked forward to being sent to do odd jobs in the barracks; plumbing or any other work that needed to be done except electrical. When the job was finished Pat and his mate were treated to tea and biscuits from Mrs Lowe the Matron. Afterwards it was back over the bridge to reality.'

Road Learning

The arrival of WR locomotives opened up the prospect of WR road learning for LMR footplatemen at Mold Junction. LMR crews would have to get to know the lines diverging to the south of Chester towards Shrewsbury, Wolverhampton and Hereford. Thus a Driver marked down for 'road learning' had to be replaced by another Driver to cover the former's normal duties and this lead to an abundance of overtime. Management worked very hard during this period in order to keep trains moving and at the same time allowing as many Drivers as could be spared to fulfil the Road Learning Programme.

The recognised way of road learning was by travelling on the train engine, standing behind the Driver and watching his every move – a very tiring thing to do. Little wonder that the twelve senior Mold Junction Drivers took the view that learning new roads, at their age, was not for them. When new rosters were introduced for 1960-61 winter working, the Top Link at Mold Junction consisted of twelve weeks work over LMR routes only. Management was displeased for it meant that there were twelve fewer Drivers available for road learning.

Wages Payment

An employee known as Jack Jones, tea maker – no one knew his proper grade – would travel by taxi every Friday to Chester General station booking office to collect the men's wages. Jack Jones was a small, dapper man who carried out this duty for many years without hiccups. Post-1960, the privilege of collecting the wages fell to George Wainwright, Foreman Cleaner. For this very important task George would don collar and tie. While George was on his way back with the money from Chester, men in the pay queue at the shed would cast anxious glances down the road lest he be delayed. If for some reason he was late, further delay would ensue while the Clerk counted the money. This system of paying out at 12.30pm on Fridays had many drawbacks. A man finishing his turn of duty at 10.00am Friday had to wait until 12.30pm for his wages. If for any reason he chose to wait until finishing his next turn of duty on Saturday morning, this could leave things late for shopping. With this in mind, the LMR staff at Mold Junction discovered that the ex-WR Chester West men were always paid on Thursdays. Later in 1960 management agreed for all staff, including Guards to be paid on Thursdays with access to wages at any time afterwards.

Personalities

Welsh sheds had a personnel problem – surnames! Most sheds had an abundance of Jones, Hughes, Roberts and so on and without nicknames confusion over who was who would have been rife. The answer was 'recognised' nicknames which were known to all and often linked to the owner's origins or some personal trait. Here are a few examples of Drivers at Mold Junction…

Driver Harry (Roman Bridge) Jones, Bill (Denbigh) Roberts, Davy (Mold) Roberts, Bill (Harbour Master) Lewis, Ted (Spouty) Jones and a Driver referred to as Brother Jones simply because he called everybody 'Brother'. Some are easy to deduce but Bill Lewis' nickname of Harbour Master came about because he lived adjacent to Connah's Quay Dock.

Railway service which spanned several generations of the same family was a common feature and Mold Junction was no exception. Father and son Drivers were Tom and Brian Caddy respectively. Tom (mentioned earlier working the Kinnerton bank engine) endured a life on the footplate with all its inherent dangers and risks. Early in his railway career he was badly injured in a collision when his light engine struck empty stock train outside Mold Junction shed in 1929. Despite severe injuries he came back to work a year later, becoming a Driver and finally retired in the late 1950s.

The Horobin brothers, all three of them, were Drivers Tom, Joe and Bert; the eldest was Tom and Bert the youngest, well known as a keen allotment gardener at his Saltney Ferry home. He was admired for his generosity as surplus vegetables would be distributed among the elderly of the village.

When Jack Chilton retired it was the end of a family era in railway history for his family spanned 98 years of railway service. Jack's grandfather had been featured with his seven sons, including his father, by a national newspaper. The paper illustrated the fact that the entire family were capable of marshalling and working a train to its destination for all were employed in various departments including

Signalman, Foreman, two Shunters, Guard, Driver, Fireman and Telephone Operator. Jack himself started as a Telephone Operator in 1929 on a wage of 16 shillings a week. Later he progressed to Supervisor at Mold Junction after being a Shunter, Guard and Foreman.

Retirement
Owen J. Hughes recalls the inevitable day before retirement: 'It was customary at 6B on a driver's last day at work to give a 'Railwaymen's Farewell' – which meant exploding detonators, sounding engine whistles and ringing the Shed Bell which hung on the shed wall between the stores entrance and the Running Shift Foreman's and Timekeeper's Office. Needless to say the locals always knew when someone retired.

'The bell with its distinctive ring, initially used by the Timekeeper for clocking on and off (there was no time clock at 6B), was also rung following an accident to alert the First Aid man on duty. Mold Junction, as did other sheds, had a first class First Aid team of volunteers; drivers, firemen, fitters and the rest were coached and advised by a local doctor. The bell was also rung, I believe, as an air raid alert during World War Two (there was a concrete air raid shelter on the coal stack side of the shed, off No.1 road). On hearing the bell all shed staff, including clerks, fitters and cleaners would assemble on the 'shed square' – woe betide anyone who rang the bell in jest.

'Retired drivers and their wives would be presented with useful gifts, a separate collection would be made for this purpose. Driver Fred Walker retired in November 1956 and was presented with a fireside chair and a handbag for Mrs Walker. During his career at 6B Fred had driven turns to Holyhead, Leeds, Buxton, Manchester, Liverpool, Birkenhead, Crewe, Denbigh and all points between.

'Driver John W. Davies also retired in 1956 after 50 years railway service. In 1938 he introduced the Mold Junction Mutual Call Club, or Sick Club. At its peak it had 238 members. Each member paid a weekly sum, collected on a Friday afternoon when most of the staff came to the shed to collect their wages. Also in attendance were Trade Union Collectors from the NUR and ASLEF.

'Another railwayman who retired in 1956 after 49 years service, 48 of which were at Mold Junction, was Yard Inspector Evelyn Wilfred Roach. He started his long railway career as a lampman and only spent one year away, at nearby Chester. He had been awarded a Long Service Medal for his St John's Ambulance duties and was also a County Council member and Elder of the Presbyterian Church, Saltney Ferry. He was involved in the Board of Managers School.'

The Barracks
No.2 Flint Road, Saltney Ferry was better known to generations of railwaymen as 'The Barracks'. The two storey building was built by the LNWR as overnight lodgings (similar accommodation was built at Holyhead, Patricroft and other key places) for Drivers, Firemen and Guards working 'double trips' or 'lodging turns' to Mold Junction from more distant locations. The accommodation provided twenty bedrooms on each landing, under the management of a Matron who had her own quarters at one end of the building. Solely gas lit, even in the 1950s, the barracks provided, on the ground floor, a mess room, kitchen (where the men had to cook their own food – crockery was provided), a bathroom, reading and billiard rooms and outside toilets. Only Matron had the luxury of a superior indoor WC.

The building was centrally heated from a free-standing coke stove in an area once used as a laundry, adjacent to the mess room. Coal and coke, ordered via the Shedmaster's office, was delivered by a wagon shunted into the Slate Yard. As part of their duties, young engine cleaners had the laborious job of wheel barrowing the fuel from wagon to the barrack's bunkers. Stray lumps of coal, deposited on the way, were quickly snatched up by children and taken home!

The Matron was on call 24 hours a day but her working hours were from 8am to 4pm Monday to Saturday- the premises were closed after the Saturday night Sunday morning shift had ended and the barracks did not reopen until 6am Monday. Up to the mid 1930s the post of Matron was held by a Mrs Fradley who moved on to the barracks at Leeds. Her place as Matron was taken by Mrs Lowe, an assistant, and she lived in and managed the Mold Junction barracks until 1955. In her day to day duties Mrs Lowe was assisted by two female assistants, the first coming on duty at 6am until 2pm, the second starting at 10am and finishing at 6pm. From that time onwards until 10pm the barracks was manned by young men primarily employed as 'knockers up'. At 10pm the 'night man' arrived and took care of any late night/early morning arrivals until 6am.

Upon entry to the barracks footplatemen and guards were required to sign the register, placed in the mess room. Lockers were provided in the kitchen to hold each man's leather basket or a guard's bag and hand lamp. At the foot of the stairs men found a large board divided up to show, by painted lines, the landings and numbered bedrooms. Every man had to select a vacant room, then in the appropriate columns on the board, enter his name, home depot or base station and the time he wished to be called. Going into his chosen quarters a man would find a small room formed by

wooden partitions reaching almost to the ceiling. The room presented a Spartan appearance; a single bed, a small wooden bench and a chamberpot were considered adequate comforts for a full eight hour's sleep. The chamberpots were emptied by staff next morning into slop sinks at the end of each landing.

Alcohol was prohibited within the building but the men, having cooked and eaten their tea or dinner, could take, depending on time of the year, an empty jug to the nearest public house. With the jug brimming with ale they would return and sit outside the barracks and pass the evening time with other lodgers and local railwaymen. Lively debate in English or Welsh might ensue over Rules and Regulations and out would come the appropriate manual to settle the argument.

Often an argument over a finer point in the rule book might be lost by a Welsh-speaking man because he spoke in English but thought in Welsh. The railway unions noted that such men, applying for promotion, would find themselves at a disadvantage when interviewed about the rule book by English management.

The more adventurous off-duty footplatemen would catch a bus or train ('on the cushions') into Chester for visits to the shops, cinema and public houses. The famous Bees Nurseries at nearby Sealand was another magnet for the many railwaymen who were keen gardeners and allotment holders. And what of the men themselves? How could they be described as they cast off their grease-top hats and deposited their bags at the barracks after a hard day or night on the footplate? Perhaps the following poem might sum them up:

'Young ones and old ones,
Timid ones and bold ones,
Short ones and tall ones,
Some drive-you-up-the-wall ones,
Thin ones and tubby ones,
A fair few of grubby ones,
Dark ones and fair ones,
Some minus-all-their-hair ones,
Happy ones and sad ones,
One or two were bad ones,
Tidy ones and scruffy ones,
Some were couldn't-care-less ones.'
Jim Lowe

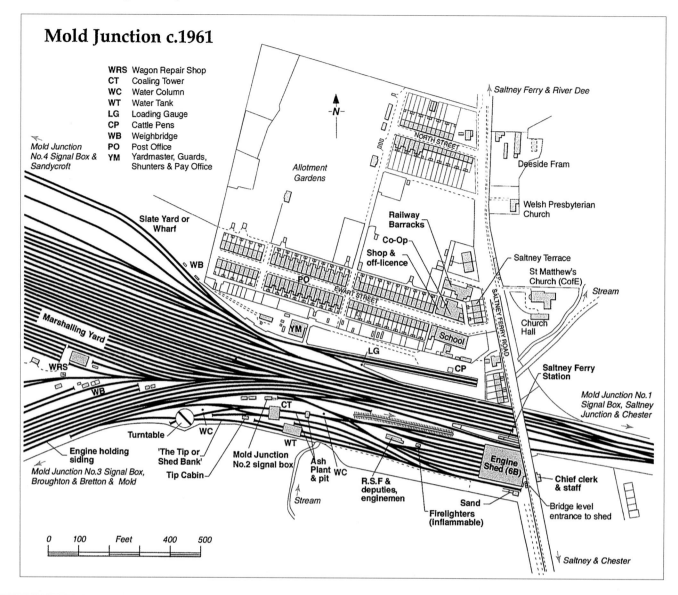

Mold Junction c.1961

WRS Wagon Repair Shop
CT   Coaling Tower
WC   Water Column
WT   Water Tank
LG   Loading Gauge
CP   Cattle Pens
WB   Weighbridge
PO   Post Office
YM   Yardmaster, Guards,
     Shunters & Pay Office

-N-

Mold Junction
No.4 Signal Box &
Sandycroft

Saltney Ferry & River Dee

Allotment
Gardens

NORTH STREET

Deeside Fram

Welsh Presbyterian
Church

Slate Yard or
Wharf

Railway
Barracks

Co-Op

Shop &
off-licence

Saltney Terrace

St Matthew's
Church (CofE)

Stream

WB

PO

EWART STREET

Church
Hall

Marshalling Yard

YM

School

SALTNEY FERRY ROAD

Saltney Ferry
Station

WRS

LG

Mold Junction No.1
Signal Box, Saltney
Junction & Chester

WB

CP

CT

Turntable

WC

Mold Junction
No.2 signal box

WT

Ash
Plant
& pit

WC

Engine holding
siding

'The Tip or
Shed Bank'

Engine
Shed (6B)

Chief clerk
& staff

Mold Junction No.3 Signal Box,
Broughton & Bretton & Mold

Tip Cabin

R.S.F &
deputies,
enginemen

Stream

Sand

Firelighters
(Inflammable)

Bridge level
entrance to shed

0   100   Feet   400   500

Saltney & Chester

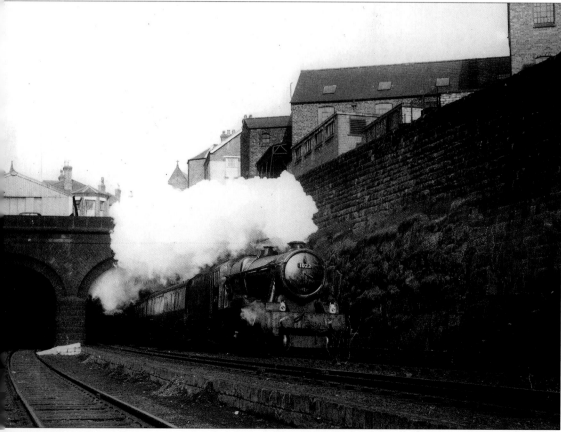

County class 4-6-0 1022 **COUNTY OF NORTHAMPTON** of Chester shed bursts out of the sandstone Northgate tunnels at Chester with a Birkenhead-Paddington express during the mid-1950s. Western Region expresses shared the same set of tracks with LMR local trains to Mold, Denbigh and Ruthin. The tracks to the left dealt with the important Chester to Holyhead traffic. In fact, at this point expresses bound for London's Paddington and Euston stations passed each other in opposite directions. Photograph Jim Peden.

Chapter Fifteen
Route Description of the Chester to Denbigh Line

The Italianate portals of Chester General station provided the setting for the beginning and end of journeys to Mold and Denbigh. Built to the design of Francis Thompson, the General station was jointly managed by the LNWR (later LMS) and the Great Western. The 'Mold Wing', located at the west end of the General station, housed platforms 1, 2 and 3. These bay platforms normally dealt with Denbigh, Paddington, Shrewsbury, Oswestry and Birkenhead Woodside trains. As a consequence this part of the joint station had a strong Great Western air but the short Platform 1 provided a contrast. Here sombre black-painted, Crewe-built tank engines fussing over a pair of crimson-lake compartment coaches made a humble comparison with the green paintwork and polished brass embellishments of Swindon-built express passenger locomotives and their chocolate and cream corridor coaches. Paddington and Denbigh departures would have one thing in common however; both services would use the down slow line for the first two miles or so out of Chester.

After departure, the Mold train would pass under Hoole road bridge, and then curve to the south-west. On the down side lay carriage storage

sidings, wagon repair shops and a goods depot while on the up side stood the GW engine shed, converted in 1960 to a diesel depot. The lines at this point formed part of a triangle, with Chester No.4 signalbox controlling traffic converging from the Birkenhead and North Wales directions. Traffic for Birkenhead not calling at Chester used the Birkenhead avoiding line which formed the third part of the triangle. Trains for Mold would then pass beneath Chester No.6 signal box which handled train movements through the western junction of the triangle.

The train then passed through Windmill Lane tunnel, a four track bore taking in both the Chester and Holyhead up and down fast lines on the right and the up and down slow lines on the left. Daylight would appear briefly before the train plunged into the twin track Northgate Street Tunnel. Reappearing, the train would skirt the red sandstone of the city walls, cross over the locks of the Shropshire Union Canal and then traverse the 49 arch Roodee Viaduct. At the beginning of the viaduct stood Crane Street signal box which signalled trains between Chester No.6 and Saltney Junction. This four track section witnessed the almost unique spectacle of Euston and Paddington expresses

passing each other, but in opposite directions.

The view from the Roodee Viaduct provided a vivid contrast; on the left-hand side the wide green sweep of Chester racecourse together with fine views of the city and cathedral while on the right lay the city gasworks. Forming a natural boundary to the racecourse, the River Dee then appeared below, the train passing over the wrought iron Dee railway bridge. This was the scene of the 1847 Dee bridge collapse which sent a Shrewsbury train plunging into the River Dee, killing six passengers and the fireman of the locomotive. The design of the original cast iron bridge, by Robert Stephenson, was found to be at fault and the subsequent findings of the public enquiry temporarily marred Stephenson's career. The bridge was extensively rebuilt in 1872 and a further two spans, added by the GWR in 1902, completed the widening to four lines, stretching from Chester to Saltney Junction. Today the Dee bridge has reverted to two; the former GW spans take both North Wales and Shrewsbury trains; the Chester and Holyhead fast lines were lifted in the late 1970s under a track and signalling modernisation scheme. Beyond Curzon Park, on Chester's southern outskirts, a deep,

Sunlight picks out the contours of both vestibuled and non-corridor LMS coaching stock, standing under the 'Mold Wing' of Chester General station. This is the old train shed, before the 1960 rebuilding work which resulted in modern canopies on the down platform. A 2-6-4T is arriving with a train from Birkenhead Woodside. Mold and Denbigh departures would normally leave from Platform 1 behind the footbridge stairs. It was in this part of Chester station that grubby LMS tank engines and immaculate GW Castle class 4-6-0s would stand together. Photograph Brian Cowlishaw.

Stanier 8F 2-8-0 48005 emerges from the sandstone Northgate Tunnel, Chester to Saltney Junction. Mold and Denbigh trains used the up and down slow lines on the right. Photograph Jim Peden.

wide cutting provides a backdrop to Saltney Junction (1m 67ch) where the GW Shrewsbury and Paddington main line diverges to the left, to the south-west. Bearing to the west, the Chester and Holyhead continued as a four track main line. At a point between Saltney and Mold Junctions, the Denbigh train would pass over the border into Wales. As if to confirm this, the distant Welsh hills appear on the left, dominated by Moel Famau (1,820ft). The lightning-blasted Jubilee Tower, standing on the summit, can be seen overlooking the more immediate industrial surroundings of Saltney. It was at Saltney that the GWR did what the LNWR failed to do; the GW tapped the coastal shipping trade of the River Dee, now visible on the left. A branch from the GW main line at Saltney passed beneath the C&H to a wharf and oil works on the river bank. Contemporary working instructions refer to the branch being restricted to the lightest of GW locomotives.

On the down or left side, Mold Junction No.1 signal box (3m 18c) marked the beginning of the Mold branch, its tracks diverging to make a total of six running lines on the approach to Saltney Ferry station (3m 37c). Here the Denbigh train would halt at an island platform, the public reaching it by stairs from the Saltney Lane overbridge.

Alongside the station stood Mold Junction engine shed. Rebuilt after World War Two from a decaying LNWR 'northlight' structure, by 1960 it had a cosmopolitan look. Green-liveried

Western Region locomotives with copper-capped chimneys and brass safety valve bonnets stood cheek by jowl with less decorative ex-LMS and BR Standard types awaiting servicing or disposal. Ex-LNER B1 4-6-0s, having

worked freights into Mold Junction from the North Eastern Region, added further variety.

Restarting from Saltney Ferry, the train curved to the south-west once more, passing on the down side the

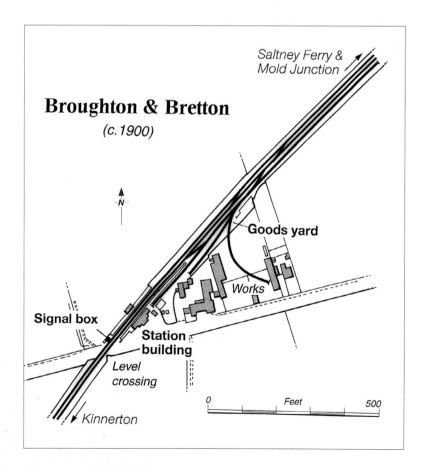

On 10 March 1958, former LNWR G2 0-8-0 49149 ambles over the Northgate locks of the Shropshire Union Canal, by the city walls at Chester. At this date these elderly locomotives were no longer allocated to Mold Junction, their heavy freight duties being taken over by more modern WD 'Austerity' and Stanier 8F 2-8-0s. Nevertheless, locomotives similar to 49149 continued to make forays through Chester to North Wales until about 1963. Photograph Jim Peden.

Left. Mold Junction 'Black 5' 4-6-0 45247 makes a vigorous start away from Saltney Junction, heading towards Chester with an up fitted freight, 10 March 1958. This locomotive spent most of its working life in North Wales. Photograph Jim Peden.

Below. Crewe South Stanier 8F 2-8-0 48255, heading a down empty cattle train, crosses the England-Wales border at Saltney on 10 March 1958. Trains to and from Denbigh used the two lines on the right. Photograph Jim Peden.

Hope & Penyffordd
(c.1912)

School

Penyffordd

-N-

Signal box

Mold

Level
crossing

Kinnerton &
Broughton &
Bretton

Penyffordd
station (GC)

**Station
building**

0   Feet   500

Wrexham

Left. Stanier Mogul 42982 of Mold Junction shed passes Saltney Junction on the down slow with a freight for Mold Junction yard on 4 October 1957. The combined home and distant arms on the right-hand bracket signal control Western Region trains bound for Wrexham, Oswestry and Shrewsbury. The left-hand bracket signal deals with traffic to Holyhead, the uppermost arm cleared for a train on the down fast line. Photograph Sidney Wainright.

Below. Having passed over the River Dee bridge, Ivatt 2-6-0 46433 of Rhyl accelerates the 10.25 Chester-Denbigh-Ruthin train through the deep cutting leading to Saltney Junction. Above the train, photographed on 25 May 1957, stands the bridge leading to Curzon Park, home of Chester Golf Club. Rhyl had an allocation of five Ivatt 2-6-0s in 1956 but they were replaced in later years by the BR Standard version. Photograph Sidney Wainright.

On a snow-blanketed day in 1955, the 10.25 Chester-Denbigh-Ruthin train, including horse box and headed by Ivatt Class 2 2-6-2T 41244, negotiates the crossover from the Chester and Holyhead down fast to slow line at Saltney Junction. Under normal conditions, Denbigh trains would use the down slow line from Chester to Mold Junction. Photograph Sidney Wainright.

Above. Hope and Penyfford, 27 August 1954. Photograph R.M. Casserley.

Left. An example of a bi-lingual L&NWR trespass sign, photographed in BR days. Interestingly the painters have seen fit not to paint out the words 'London and North Western Railway'. Photograph Author's Collection.

Llong station looking east. Chester's BR Class 4 2-6-4T 80051 pulls away with the 12.45pm Saturdays only Chester-Denbigh on 2 August 1958. The low height of the platforms in relation to the carriage stepboards is noteworthy. 80051 was based at Chester from January 1957 to May 1960 and then moved to Scotland. Photograph H.B. Priestley.

turntable, coaling tower and Mold Junction No.2 signal box. This controlled entry to the shed and to the marshalling yard on the right. With a capacity for 900 wagons, Mold Junction yard sorted and exchanged wagon load traffic to and from North Wales with that from the Midlands and North of England. Beyond the C&H main line, further sidings specialised in sorting wagon loads of slate from the North Wales quarries.

Once clear of the main part of the yard the train passed Mold Junction No.3 signal box. This controlled entry to Mold Junction from the Mold direction together with a south to west curve; thus seaside excursion traffic could run direct from Mold to Prestatyn, Rhyl, Colwyn Bay and Llandudno. The Denbigh train now crossed over land that once lay beneath the sea. In the eighteenth century the River Dee was canalised, from Shotton to form land suitable for farming. This flat land, ideal for laying out Mold Junction yard, also proved suitable for building an aerodrome and as the Denbigh train neared Broughton & Bretton station, Hawarden airfield appeared on the right-hand side. It was opened in 1939 and jointly used by the RAF on the Hawarden or west side of the aerodrome and Vickers, who occupied the factory on the Broughton or east side. The airfield served for

many years as a training and aircraft storage base and scores of war surplus aircraft were visible from the train in the immediate post war years. Some almost brand new, they stood wing to wing, awaiting scrapping. Transferred to the de Havilland Aircraft Company in 1948, the Broughton factory recommenced aircraft production and throughout the 1950s and 1960s produced hundreds of aircraft including a batch of the famous Comet 4 jet airliner for the state-run British Overseas Airways Corporation.

Between Saltney Ferry and Broughton and Bretton, the Mold branch gradient dipped to 1 in 660 and then ran level before rising gently to 1 in 270 on the approach to Broughton and Bretton station (4m 54c). On the up side were the Ministry of Aircraft Production sidings which led into the Broughton factory, while on the down side lay further private sidings, occupied in 1960 by the Premier Artificial Stone Company. The station goods yard closed to general freight traffic on 5th May 1964 except for wagons using the

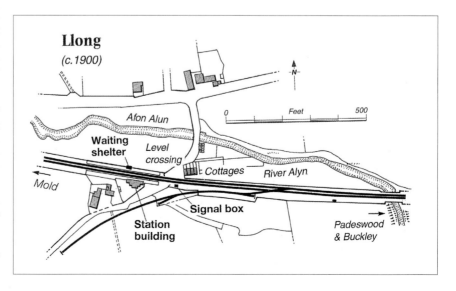

The A541 level crossing at Rhydymwyn in BR days, with the station platform on the left. The absence of any road traffic, which led to the closure of the line, is only too noticeable. Photograph Glyn Morris.

A member of the station staff opens the level crossing gates to road traffic on the A541 at Rhydymwyn, 21 April 1962. A group of visiting railway enthusiasts, anxious to travel the line before its closure, shelter from the rain as they await the next train. Photograph Author's Collection.

Top. Rhydymwyn station, looking towards Dolfeshlas Crossing and Hendre. This is after the withdrawal of passenger services but the station and signalling remain intact with both lines still in use for freight traffic, mainly limestone from the Hendre quarries. The bracket signal combines Dolfechlas Crossing down distant arm with Rhydymwyn's home starter signal.

Left. Brighton-built Standard Class 4 2-6-4T 80091 slows to a halt at Star Crossing with the 11.41am 3-coach Ruthin to Chester on 2 August 1958. Despite the modern concrete platform supports and paving slabs the halt retains oil lamps. A Mold Junction fireman recalled having to 'put your boot out to find the platform edge' on foggy or moonless nights to draw the train up safely, such was the low level of lighting on rural stations and halts even in the 1950s. 80091 ended its days far from rural Wales at Hurlford, near Kilmarnock. Photograph H.B. Priestley.

Below. Driver's eye view of Nannerch station. Passengers await the Chester-bound service. The engine is passing over the horse landing dock points. Photograph Brian Cowlishaw.

Nannerch station, looking east, on 21 April 1962. A pair of 16 ton wagons that have brought in domestic coal can be seen beyond the up platform. A Ford Prefect stands behind the station nameboard. Photograph Author's Collection.

Nannerch station, looking westwards towards the A541 road bridge, on 21 April 1962. Apart from the raised concrete platforms built by the LMS and the modern upper-quadrant signals little else has changed over the years. Closure was but a week away. Photograph Author's Collection.

Nannerch station exudes a deserted air as Rhyl's Ivatt Class 2 2-6-0 46445 stands at the up platform with a Chester train, about 1958. Photograph N.R. Knight.

private sidings. After making its booked stop at Broughton and Bretton the train immediately crossed the A55 Chester to Bangor road. Its level crossing gates were open and shut from the signal box adjoining the up platform.

From the carriage compartment, the locomotive's exhaust would have been heard to sharpen as the engine tackled the next mile of rising gradients, 1 in 76 and 92 and then easing to 1 in 384 before falling gently at 1 in 325 to a point prior to Kinnerton station (6m 23c). Situated near the border between England and Wales, the station served both Higher Kinnerton and Lower Kinnerton villages. The modest goods yard dealt mainly with livestock and closed on 5th December 1955. The view from the carriage window would have been pleasantly rural as the engine restarted on Kinnerton bank, passing under the distinctive double-arched road overbridge at Higher Kinnerton. The wide expanse of fields forming the Cheshire Plain stretched away to the east; ahead, on the left-hand side, loomed the steep sides of Hope Mountain while on the right the ground rose more gently towards Little Mountain and the town of Buckley.

For the next two and a half miles the Mold branch climbed continuously on an embankment, the gradient sharpening from 1 in 63 to 1 in 55 and then steeply at 1 in 43. Having passed through a deep cutting and Dodd's Sand

Siding on the left, the line then began to curve west and then north-west as the train crossed the 200ft Ordnance Survey datum. For the next mile the uphill grades began to ease from 1 in 50 to 1 in 124, the line passing over further embankments and cuttings. A short section of level track provided a brief respite before a further half mile climb of 1 in 124 brought the train,

heading west once more, to Hope and Penyffordd station (8m 79ch). Sidings existed on both the up and down side of the line, having a capacity for 6 and 16 wagons respectively. These closed with effect from 9th September 1955. At the Mold end of the station stood a wartime brick-built ARP signalbox which controlled the level crossing gates across the A550 Wrexham to Birkenhead road.

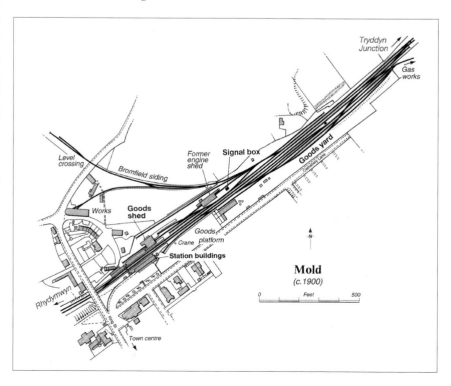

Caerwys station on a damp Saturday, 21 April 1962. Compared with other intermediate stations between Mold and Denbigh, Caerwys is well-equipped with a goods shed and private as well as railway-owned sidings. By now, unfortunately, goods traffic had virtually ceased. Photograph Author's Collection.

BR Standard Class 4MT 4-6-0 75010 departs from Caerwys with an up Chester train, on a very damp Saturday afternoon, 21 April 1962. Photograph Author's Collection.

Portrait of a LNWR up home signal at Caerwys. Photograph I. Vaughan.

Junction. A siding once led north to the Nant Branch Colliery Co., the rails crossing the Mold to Penyffordd road. From Ffrith Junction the line began to rise once more to reach Padeswood & Buckley station (10m 64ch). It was well equipped for handling goods traffic, the yard possessing a crane and goods shed. Yet Padeswood, once a centre for the oil and coal industry, lost all importance when both industries collapsed. Passengers alighting for the more important town of Buckley faced a mile-long, uphill walk to reach the town. To the north of the station was a pit from which the LNWR extracted ballast but by 1876 this had been worked out.

For the next two and a half miles the line continued gently climbing to reach Mold but before that the train would have called at Llong station (11m 53ch). Closed for the first time on January 1st 1917, the wayside station, which served but a few cottages, reopened on May 5th 1919. Before reaching the station, the cast iron girders of Llong Bridge carried the rails over the River Alyn, a tributary of the River Dee. The station once had private sidings; according to an 1876 survey 'Mrs Prudence Wynn & Others', owned a siding parallel to the main line while a Mr Thompson owned sidings which curved away behind the station building.

Between Llong and Mold the line swung to the north-west, re-crossing the River Alyn twice in quick succession before reaching Mold & Tryddyn Junction. The gradient rose from 1 in 560 to 1 in 258. Nearing the latter junction, the single track Coed Talon branch, on a low embankment, became visible on the left or down side. The branch, on a falling grade from Coed Talon, merged with the Mold line through a set of catch points, overlooked by Mold & Tryddyn Junction signal box. Dating from 1875, the 24 lever Saxby & Farmer structure closed, after a life of ninety years, on 28th February 1967. It outlived the Coed Talon branch by being responsible for controlling road traffic crossing the Mold branch via Gas Lane.

Sidings appeared to both left and right as the driver braked to bring the train to a stand at Mold (13m 25ch), the largest intermediate station between Chester and Denbigh. Beyond the Chester end of the platforms stood a brick-built wartime ARP signal box, on the left or down side of the line. There was a large brick goods shed immediately behind the station on the up or Chester side. Beyond that stood the former engine shed, converted to a grain store and stables. A lengthy siding owned by J.A. Hughes of Altami, curved northwards through the goods yard and at one time crossed Chester Street; this siding was also known as Mold Argoed Siding.

The Chester Street overbridge (a convenient vantage point for the stonethrowers at Mold station during

Beyond Hope and Penyfordd station the train continued to climb at 1 in 124 for half a mile to reach Hope Low Level. Before that, the abandoned earthworks of the former WM&CQ south to east curve were to be seen on the down side. Hope Low Level (9m 30ch) existed in the middle of a field with no external road access. Only a footpath connected the low level platforms, at right angles, to the High Level station. After restarting under the bridge the train reached its first summit as the south to west spur from the WM&CQ came in from the left. There were several sidings here for the exchange of goods traffic while on the up side of the Mold branch stood Hope Junction signalbox. Behind the box lay more abandoned earthworks, the remnants of a west to north spur which would have given

through running from Mold to Buckley Junction and beyond.

Speed would quicken as the gradient began to fall for the next mile, descending first at 1 in 108 and 1 in 94 before crossing Wat's Dyke; as the line levelled out at 1 in 380 it passed the site, on the down side, of Ffrith Junction and the branch of that name. In 1956, the long-abandoned and overgrown site of Ffrith Junction (also known as Padeswood & Buckley Junction) would have given little clue as to the intensity of coal and oil traffic of ninety years before. Tank wagons, carrying oil distilled from coal at Coppa, Padeswood and Coed Talon, would have filled the storage sidings on the branch while awaiting transit to Saltney, Bagillt and Queensferry for further refining. Further activity occurred on the up side of Ffrith

Peaceful Caerwys station, 5 May 1961. A number of engineering wagons, loaded with ballast, stand in the platform siding. Otherwise there is no evidence of ordinary wagonload traffic in the goods yard although the local timber merchant has plenty of work in hand. The station running-in board appears to be new, the posts lacking the customary coat of (peeling!) crimson and cream paint. Beyond the station on the down side stands the buildings and chimney; the Ordnance Survey recorded this site in 1913 as an 'iron foundry'. Photograph Author's Collection.

On a very wet 21 April 1962, Llandudno Junction's Standard class 4MT 75010 is about to pass under the A541 bridge at Bodfari with a down Denbigh train. Photograph Keith Smith.

The porter/signalman at Bodfari raises his arm to take the single line token from the crew of a dirty BR Standard Class 4 4-6-0 as it draws to a halt at the up platform with a Chester-bound train on a very wet Saturday, 21 April 1962. Photograph G. Harrop.

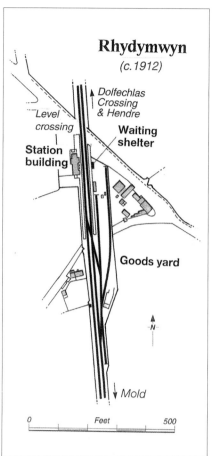

Passengers walk past Rhyl's Ivatt 2-6-2T 41232, after arrival at Denbigh in the early 1950s; the engine is halted alongside the Wymans bookstall, still open for business. A tank wagon, used for removing tar from the town gas works, stands in the siding opposite. Photograph AWV Mace Collection.

A Compound 4-4-0 leaves Denbigh for Ruthin, photographed from a bridge near Clywedog, Ruthin Road on 17 August 1949. Photograph D.S. Foulkes-Roberts.

The fireman of BR Standard Class 4MT 4-6-0 75033 and a Chester-bound train at Ruthin, April 1962. Photograph Brian Cowlishaw.

the 1869 riot) heralded the beginning of the erstwhile Mold & Denbigh Junction Railway. When it opened, Mold was transformed from branch terminus to a through station. In the centre of the bridge, on the station side, was a stone plaque with 1866 in raised numerals. This date reflected the hopes of the M&DJ promoters in opening the line that year. But it was to be a further three years before trains actually steamed beneath the bridge upon departure for Denbigh.

Yr Wyddgrug, the Welsh name for Mold is derived from Wytgruc, the 'Wyt' being a contraction of 'gwydd' a burial mound, the final resting place of Gruc. Yr Wyddgrug is also thought to mean 'forest heath', recalling the time when much of the area was heavily forested. The English name 'Mold' dates from the Norman invasion. The town itself lies at the junction of roads radiating out to Chester, Wrexham, Connah's Quay, Buckley, Ruthin and Denbigh and always seems to have done, even as far back as Roman times. A Roman road to Conovium (Conwy) passed close by.

Mold, in modern times, has become the marketplace for agricultural and

industrial life in the Alun Valley as well as, by the 1970s, the important administrative and cultural centre for the county of Clwyd. By that time Mold had little to show of its former importance as a coal-producing town. Only the statue of Daniel Owen, 19th century novelist and social critic, reminded townsfolk of a recent, turbulent industrial past. Owen wrote of the struggles of ordinary working people and the birth of trade unionism, both of which were profoundly felt in Mold. In doing so, Owen was assured an important place in Welsh literature. Perhaps it was no coincidence that his statue, until relocated in a town centre redevelopment plan, looked out over Mold Station approach road, scene of the 1869 riots.

Having departed from Mold the train passed beneath both Chester and King Street bridges in quick succession. The line continued a north-westerly alignment, a stone retaining wall running along the down side as it emerging from the town. The train then passed under Milford Street footbridge, the alignment now curving to the west on a subtle, rising gradient of 1 in 368. From the

carriage window, the town buildings began to thin out to open fields but, dominating the skyline to the south of Mold, are the slopes of the 1,820 ft Moel Famau (Mother of Mountains) and highest point in the Clwydian range of hills. (Moel Famau qualifies as a mountain by 20 feet). The first month of the Mold Railway's existence brought an excursion train from Chester, whose occupants were intent on climbing Moel Famau. Alas the rain, true to form, intervened! Now much closer, the mountain complemented the town's principal landmarks of the elevated 15th century parish church of St Mary's and ancient Bailey Hill. A 19th century colliery known as Bedford Pits enjoyed a brief existence on this, the west side of Mold. A signal box on the left-hand or down side of the line controlled access to the colliery. Little trace remained of the spur, even by 1900.

The River Alyn or Alun re-appeared to the right of the train as the Alyn Tin Plate Sidings signalbox came into view, also on the right. To the left, tank wagons stood in the sidings belonging to Synthite Ltd. After the factory had passed by, the River Alyn flowed

42540 approaches Clywedog bridge with train from Ruthin to Denbigh on 17 August 1949. Photograph D.S. Foulkes-Roberts.

beneath the railway to re-emerge on the left-hand side. It accompanied the railway for the next two miles to Rhydymwyn where the river course turned southwards to its source near Llantysilio Mountain, overlooking the Vale of Llangollen. Immediately after crossing the River Alyn, the train passed under the A541 road bridge at Rhyd-y-Goleu, before line entered a sweeping curve to the west. The gradients along this section of track, between Mold and Rhydymwyn, were undemanding, ranging from 1 in 561 to 1 in 184.

On the approach to Rhydymwyn the sides of the Alyn valley narrowed briefly as the line curved once more to the north-west. A deep cutting on the right at Bellan quickly passed by while on the left the first buildings of the extensive government-owned Valley Works ordnance factory came into view. Reception sidings for the factory appeared, segregated from the Denbigh line by a high steel fence. On a section of level track, the train then drew to a stand at Rhydymwyn station (16m 25ch), with the station goods yard on the right. Rhydymwyn signal box stood some way from the station in the Mold direction. A modern steel bracket signal protected the level crossing immediately at the platform end. The A541 Mold-Trefnant road crossed the line here and would run in close proximity to the

Mold-Denbigh line as far as Bodfari. The village lay to the left; the name was derived from 'Rhyd' which means 'ford' and 'mwyn' meaning 'mine'.

Leaving Rhydymwyn, the train ran over a straight, low embankment as far as Dolfechlas Crossing signal box where the line entered the hills at the head of the Alyn valley. Beyond the signal box at Dolfechlas stood the buildings and chimneys of the Ruby Brickworks, which nestled in a cleft at the foot of Halkyn Mountain, on the right-hand side of the train. Having passed the brickworks and its sidings, the railway curved sharply to the west again, on a gradient of 1 in 94 in order to take the railway over the A541, as there was little space at ground level for both. Further sidings appeared on the right as the train passed the extensive quarries at Hendre. From here loaded wagons would take crushed limestone to industry in the north-west of England. Wagonload traffic from Hendre once brought in the highest level of freight receipts over the whole line from Mold Junction to Denbigh. On the left side of the train lay Halkyn sidings and the modest, wooden-built signal box of the same name. Below it, at the foot of the embankment, lay the village of Hendre, clustered along the main road, over which the train had just passed twice in quick succession.

The train continued to head west and passed along a heavily-wooded section of line cut into the hillside. The landscape then began to open out once more and the rural nature of the surrounding countryside manifested itself. This was a North Wales landscape of hillside farms and narrow, hedged lanes, a far cry from the jagged peaks of Snowdonia, some thirty miles distant. The gentle slopes of Moel Arthur could be seen on the left. At a height of 1,492ft Moel Arthur was another peak, like Moel Famau, in the Clwydian chain of hills. Although lower in height, Moel Arthur was no less interesting; ditches near the summit, whose edges had been rounded with the passing of time, gave life to its ancient role as a hill fort. Hidden beyond Moel Arthur's flanks, to the south-west, lay the town of Ruthin, the train's eventual destination.

The train now reached the line's second and final summit of 534 feet above sea level, just short of Star Crossing Halt. From Mold the line had risen continuously for six miles, the last two at gradients of 1 in 94, 97 and 92. Star Crossing Halt (18m 55ch) lay alongside the A541 and from here the halt served the village of Cilcain, three miles distant through country lanes to the south, at the foot of Moel Famau. From Star Crossing Halt the crew would have relaxed as the next eight miles were all on falling grades, the line now turning north-west to descend into the Wheeler valley, whose river would form a tributary to the River Clwyd. There would be no opportunity for the train crew to gain any lost time for, little more than a mile from Star Crossing, the brakes would go on once more for the approach to Nannerch Station, on a falling grade of 1 in 80.

Like the adjacent A541 main road, Nannerch Station (19m 48ch) did not directly serve Nannerch village. The village stood at a higher level half a mile away, linked by a minor road. The name Nannerch is a combination of the word 'nant' meaning stream and 'erch', coloured. A single siding behind the up or Mold-bound platform served the local community, domestic coal being the main commodity. In the line's heyday, much of the wagonload traffic would have been concerned with the maintenance of the Penbedw Estate which lay to the south-west of the station, beyond the A541. A further siding, past the station, served as a horse landing. In the 1950s the staff, station master and porter/signalman, would have operated the signals and points from the ground frame on the platform. Between passenger trains, the daily pick up goods was allowed ten minutes to shunt wagons at Nannerch.

Having pulled away from Nannerch, and passing under the A541 road bridge, the line curved gently due north and then north-west on descending gradients of 1 in 73, 114, 78 and 83 for the next three miles to Caerwys. The railway entered a short but deep cutting; above, an iron bridge carrying a minor road from Nannerch village dropped steeply to meet the A541 road, now on the right. Beyond the bridge the A541 ran in close proximity to the railway, both traversing the floor of the Wheeler valley. A high limestone wall shielded road from rail traffic but the origin of the wall goes back to the line's early days, before the advent of the motor-car, when cart horses had to be protected from bolting at the sight and sound of a passing 'iron horse', only feet away.

To the north of the railway and above on the hillside lay the village of Ysceifiog. Below it a large lake contained fish hatcheries. Known as the 'Fisheries', the lake, bounded by woods dotted with footpaths, became popular with day excursionists and ramblers from Cheshire and Merseyside. Such travellers would alight at Caerwys, the next booked stop.

Caerwys station (23m 1ch) was some distance from the town. 'Caer' means a fortified place and in the Roman times Caerwys (or Caerwis), owing to its elevated position, was a signal station. In more recent times it became an important stopping and meeting place for drovers on their trek to the English cattle markets, Caerwys lying at the meeting place of roads from Denbigh,

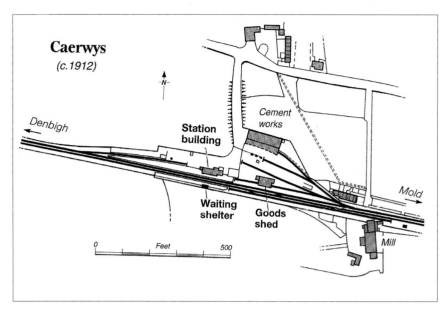

Caerwys
(c.1912)

Denbigh

Station
building

Cement
works

Mold

Waiting
shelter

Goods
shed

Mill

0   Feet   500

Mold, St Asaph and Holywell. The coming of the railway brought the drover traffic to an end. Although giving the appearance of a village, Caerwys is in fact a town, having been given borough status by Edward 1 in 1290.

The station was well equipped for goods traffic with sidings on both sides of the running lines. A goods shed, on the up side, handled general traffic while the British Portland Cement Manufacturers Ltd had their own premises furthest from the station but sharing the same road access. Other individuals had their own private sidings; in 1956 Mr G.A. Rees was using a siding previously belonging to a Mr A. J. Martin. Another was owned by Mr J. Charmley and is recorded as such by the Railway Clearing House in 1938. Caerwys's private siding traffic had all but vanished by 1960 and the owners raised no objection when closure notices came. Three separate ground frames, released by an Annetts key, controlled point movements in the sidings and crossover while on the up station platform an exposed eight lever frame worked the signals.

Caerwys station stood on the level but the erstwhile Mold and Denbigh Junction Railway resumed its descent in the Wheeler valley, continuing to follow a north-westerly course for the next mile and a half on a falling gradient of 1 in 73, 112, 103 and 106. The train criss-crossed the River Wheeler several times and then, together with adjacent river and A541 road, curved sharply to the south-west, breaking through the Clwydian hills to reach the Vale of Clwyd. The locality is sometimes referred to as the Pass of Agricola, recalling its earlier use by the Romans. On the left lay Moel-y-Parc (1,305ft) whose generous slopes and position would lead, in the 1960s, to the installation of a more modern form of communication – a television transmitter mast. On the right stood Moel-y-Gaer (672ft), another ancient hill fort, overlooking Bodfari village.

The line assumed a more westerly course as the train, on a curve, passed under the A541 and came to a halt, on the level, in Bodfari station (25m 47ch). The 'Bod' in Bodfari means dwelling place and 'fari' is said to originate from Varis, a nearby Roman settlement. The village of Bodfari overlooked the station with St Stephen's church dominating the skyline. Dr Johnson, who worshipped there while on his Welsh journeyings, was complimentary about the standard of sermon, administered both in English and Welsh.

Like Nannerch and Caerwys, no signalbox was ever provided at Bodfari. There was instead an eight lever ground frame, exposed to the elements, on the up platform. These levers controlled only the signals. The signalling block instruments, operated by the porter/ signalman, were kept in an office within the station building. Access to the goods yard, on the up side, was from a two lever ground frame, released by Annetts key. In 1912 a single siding, with access at both ends, was sufficient for goods traffic. With the beginning in 1923 of the Partington Steel Company's quarrying activities the siding layout was changed and enlarged to provide rail access for their wagonload traffic. In the goods yard a five ton crane was available for general merchandise and the loading dock was equipped to handle livestock. For a brief period in the early 1950s the old Partington sidings were revived by Mr Pennant; the family name had been associated with railways at Bodfari ever since the line opened in 1869. When the line was singled from Bodfari to Denbigh in 1957 the station ground frame was adapted to work the necessary pointwork at the west end of the station. Drivers and firemen handed in or picked up the electric token for the single line section from the station staff.

For the next mile and a quarter to the Blue Hand road overbridge, the railway continued on a dead straight alignment, through a lengthy cutting and over an embankment, the most visible and permanent feature of the railway in the locality. A footbridge, known locally as the 'Pandy Bridge' straddled the cutting; this took a footpath from Bodfari to Pontruffyd Farm, on the south side of the railway. The Roman settlement of Varis is supposed to lie close by to Pontruffyd Farm but the precise location has led to much debate, over the years, by historians.

For a further mile the railway continued to descend, on a grade of 1 in 109, the embankment abutting an attractive three-arch limestone bridge which took the rails over the winding River Clwyd. The Vale of Clwyd at this point is at its widest and presents a spectacle of flat meadows adjoining the river bank, the Clwydian range of hills a distant backdrop.

A mile and a half from Bodfari the train passed under the Blue Hand bridge, which had to be taken down and rebuilt when work on the Mold & Denbigh Junction Railway was almost finished. The bridge took the A541 over the railway, for the last time, northwards towards Trefnant and Rhyl. The railway then curved sharply to the south-west on a rising grade of 1 in 96 to meet the former Vale of Clwyd Railway whose rails appeared on the right. Although giving the impression of a two-track railway the rails to Rhyl were only double for a short distance north of Mold & Denbigh Junction signal box (28m 21ch). The train passed the signal box on the right; this 1894-built standard Composite 4 LNWR structure (a replacement for an earlier box dating from 1880) possessed a 20 lever frame for controlling the divergence of the Rhyl and Mold routes. It signalled its last train in April 1957 and was demolished after the Rhyl and Mold lines converged on Denbigh for just over a mile as separate, single tracks.

Now headed south over the old Vale of Clwyd Railway the county town of Denbigh could be seen rising up to the right of the train, topped by the ruins of the 13th Century castle, with its commanding view of the vale. A more recent earthwork on the left, destined never to carry the weight of a train, was the abandoned Mold & Denbigh Junction Railway embankment, a grassy memorial to the Mold company's independent attempt to reach Denbigh while in conflict with the dominant LNWR.

On the outskirts of Denbigh the rails, on a gentle descent of 1 in 1,079, passed over the A525 Rhyl to Wrexham road. Denbigh engine shed appeared on the left, home to a handful of tank and secondary main line locomotives. Whitewashed bricks, laid out on a shallow embankment spelt out the words 'DENBIGH' at the entrance to the shed. To the right the tracks fanned out into Denbigh goods yard as the train passed through Denbigh station (29m 27ch). A single siding rose up on an embankment and curved away to serve the Craig Lelo quarry. On the left, sidings served the town gas works, wedged between the railway and the A525.

Having come to a rest beyond Vale Street bridge, to the south of the station, the locomotive then reversed the coaches into the single, through platform. Above, the station's spire gave the place the appearance, from the approach road, of a country school but the structure was quite in keeping with Denbigh's status as a 'country junction'. A low curved platform canopy gave shelter from the weather. The Welsh spelling for Denbigh is Dinbych, 'Din' meaning enclosed, safe place, and 'bych' derived from 'bach', a small place. Welsh is the everyday language in Denbigh but the town was English inspired, owing much to the building of the castle in 1282 by Edward I as part of his campaign of conquest. The town was then contained within the castle walls but the locality had a violent history, the fortress being briefly captured by the Welsh 1294. During the War of the Roses the town became a Yorkist stronghold and in their quest to take the castle, the town was burnt down by the Lancastrians. It was subsequently rebuilt outside the castle walls. The English Civil War of 1643-1648 did not leave the castle unscathed either; after his defeat near Chester, Charles I spent three days at the castle in September 1645. The following year, under the command of Colonel Salusbury, it withstood a six month siege by Cromwell's Parliamentary forces. Only the relative isolation of the garrison led to its eventual surrender, the castle then becoming a prison for captured Royalists. Thereafter it fell into ruin until taken over by the Commissioner of Works in 1914. Latterly Cadw, (Welsh Historic Monuments) on behalf of the Secretary of State for Wales, has taken care of Denbigh Castle. Owing to its elevated position, with the town centre beneath it, the local saying has it that, 'if in doubt, go uphill'. To a railway passenger, having just walked out of the station into Vale Street, at the foot of the town, the advice was perfectly sound.

Looking over his or her shoulder, the erstwhile passenger would watch the train rumble over Vale Street bridge, continuing its journey over the single track of the former Denbigh, Ruthin and Corwen Railway, calling at Rhewl (34m 40ch) and Ruthin (35m 79ch). The view from the carriage on that part of the line offered superb views of the Clwydian range of hills, now seen from the south-west, rich in a diversity of colour according to season and topped by Moel Famau, whose windswept summit had watched over the train's progress all the way from Chester.